BETWEEN THE BROKEN GLASS THE PEOPLE

PLAY

A Sixties Love Story

Christine Day

Shattering the fragile boundary between passion and abuse

ETHERIC BOOKS

People believe that if you can remember the Sixties then you weren't really there. But I remember, vividly……how could I possibly forget?

BETWEEN THE BROKEN GLASS THE PEOPLE PLAY is the true story of a young journalist whose colourful lifestyle, reporting on the Sixties pop scene in London, is overshadowed by her poignant and dramatic love affair with an actor who has suffered an excruciating breakdown.

Living in the eye of a cultural revolution – rubbing shoulders with icons such as the Beatles, the Rolling Stones, the Who, Dylan and Jimi Hendrix – she struggles to survive this heart-breaking entanglement and somehow heal it.

Fragment One: Pop Stars

KEN Walmsley, editor of the pop magazine Boyfriend, is deaf. He is slumped over his desk with his head on his hands, crying...

His assistant, Maggie Koumi, sits at another desk a short distance away. Her enormous brown eyes reflect his sorrow. She mouths words to him slowly and with such exaggeration that her battery appears to be flat. One day in the distant future she will be the editor of *Hello!* magazine and one of the most highly regarded editors in London.

In the adjoining office Patsy Chapman, a tiny, frail girl in her teens is sorting through a tray of readers' letters. Her hair is drawn into a knot at the nape of her neck, and she has a deep fringe. She is as fizzy as lemonade and deceptively childlike. One day she will be the editor of *The News of the World.* The office boy, Mick Gill, is tall, skinny, hyper. He has his own column in the magazine and is worshipped by thousands of schoolgirls. Soon he will leave to become Rod Stewart's PA and be interviewed wearing fur coats, at airports.

Up several flights of stairs, in a small office, Claire Rayner, who is destined to become a famous agony aunt, is working on a magazine for young mums with babies. The reception is in the charge of an empathetic, dizzy blonde. Shirley trips around in stilettos and the tightest of skirts, dragging on endless cigarettes as she connects the most influential figures on the pop scene into various phones around the building. She came in one morning, whiter than a sheet after her fiancé dumped her. She is not as dizzy as she seems.

The reporters work in an office adjoining the reception. Above the ornate fireplace, which is filled with a gas fire, is a large mirror. Legendary pop stars warm their hands and comb their hair when they emerge for interviews from the chaos of chilly Oxford Street.

One of the reporters, Sue Mautner, is dating Rolling Stone, Brian Jones. He calls in to pick her up, blond hair almost touching his shoulders, wearing a wide-brimmed, beige hat and an enigmatic smile. Not far in the future he will be found dead in a swimming pool, a founder member of the ill-fated 27 Club.

Sue behaves more like a model than a journalist. She always carries a bag with a change of clothes, false hair pieces, and make-up brushes. Soon she will be sacked when she is discovered by Reg Taylor, the managing director, sitting at her desk with her dark red hair pinned up in rollers.

I am the other reporter. I have arrived here by what seemed to be an accident. I applied for a position editing a baby magazine, advertised in a tiny box in *The Evening Standard*. At the interview I had pretended to be interested in babies, but Claire Rayner had obviously been far more convincing. Instead, I am offered a job on the company's pop magazine.

Within days I am an integral part of the London pop scene. People call me when they need publicity. I am suddenly powerful, can make or break with a few, carefully chosen words.

Tall, slim – much slimmer than a year ago – I am wearing a dark pink, needle-cord mini skirt, slung low on the hips, with a wide, matching, belt. A black, ribbed skinny sweater with three-quarter length sleeves and a scooped neckline is tucked inside. They were purchased at the Oxford Street branch of trendy high street chain *Neatawear*. The hem of my skirt is four inches above my knees. The first mini skirt I wore, a few weeks ago, was only two inches above and caused a sensation. Things are moving fast. There is a fashion revolution. Sheer black tights fill the gap between the hem and the tops of my white Courrèges *boots*. My dark brown hair is cut in a glossy Egyptian bob. I go regularly to *Evansky*, a hairdressers on par with *Vidal Sassoon*, known for their superb cut. The stylist cellotapes my hair across my cheeks when it is being blow dried, so that the bangs stay flat and pointed.

When I joined the magazine my hair was halfway down my back. *Tony, my boyfriend, twisted it into a rope.*

The magazine offices are in Mayfair in an attractive red brick terrace in North Audley Street, near Selfridges. The dark room is in the cellar and the art room in the attic. The favourite spot for photo shoots is out on the roof.

My loss of weight is due to a number of factors; the speed at which I live; the countless cigarettes I smoke; my love life. The latter is so intense and unpredictable I am hardly ever in a calm state.

I am expected to produce a number of features for the magazine each week. I start typing on Monday morning, after the editorial meeting, and keep going until Friday afternoon.

Reg Taylor pops his head round the door to tell me how *impressed* he is with my work. I'm not amazingly paid, £11 a week, cash in an envelope.

My last job as a reporter on a weekly newspaper paid five pounds ten shillings a week. So this is a vast improvement. We all fiddle expenses, in order to survive, charging for fictitious lunches and taxi fares. I travel all over London in taxis to attend lavish receptions for pop stars being launched by record companies. Sometimes I invade as many as three a day, carrying impressive invitations edged with gold. These flood in through the post

3

and are immediately made a note of in the large diary sitting on Ken's desk. There are also invitations to film previews at plush mini cinemas in Soho where drinks are served before the screening. There is often a rising star in the dark observing his or her performance.

Ken and I will become close friends, but this is taking time. We are tuning in to each other's tragedy slowly. But I always feel a flood of warmth coming from his heart. He is such a spontaneous man, quite different from Reg Taylor, his business partner. When I approach Reg for a rise he attempts to make me feel guilty.

Ken is lean and wears loose-fitting, grey suits. He is endlessly searching his pockets for book matches and his fingers are stained with nicotine. He is alive as an exposed wire and eternally frustrated by his deafness which makes him shout. His Scots accent is grating and unforgettable. It stays in my head like a love song.

He lost his hearing during the war. He served in the navy and his ship was torpedoed. He was rushed to a hospital and the building was bombed. He has that sort of luck. After the war he returned to Fleet Street. He is really an ideas man. He helped create *Dennis the Menace* and *Biffo the Bear*. The publishers he worked for in Dundee, let him go, apparently because his politics were too left-wing.

He is crying. His head is in his hands. His sixteen-year-old son has been killed in a road accident. He bought him a motorbike for his birthday. The first time he rode it he was hit by a lorry. When the headmaster had complained about the length of his son's hair, Ken grew his own before going to see him. The compassionate assistant editor is holding everything together while Ken grieves. I catch a glimpse of Ken at his desk. I cannot imagine his pain. He has no choice but to accept it like another confusing, Oxford Street morning.

He senses where I'm coming from, my silhouette blurred by his tears. Later he will write me poems that he stuffs in his pockets along with the book matches.

I am twenty and don't realise how young I am. It feels as if it has taken an extremely long climb to reach this point in my life. It is early spring 1965. I joined the magazine several months ago and was thrown in at the deep end. But unlike Brian Jones I didn't drown. I find myself backstage at concerts, interviewing newly famous pop groups I know little about, let alone how to handle their quips. The greatest challenge is remembering all their names. I get the hang of it. I have to.

Cliff Richard, starring in Aladdin at the London Palladium with the Shadows, welcomes me into his dressing room before he goes on stage. The Christmas panto is a sell-out. He is wearing a robe and slippers, and is terribly polite and well-mannered. He asks me if I smoke and produces an enormous glass ashtray. Cliff makes me feel remarkably at ease. I had a huge crush on him when I was fourteen. I take some of his sparkle out into the shadowy Piccadilly streets.

Ken compensates for his deafness with a keen insight into the pop scene. He knows who is talented. He has a gut feeling which has never let him down. He is particularly proud of his relationship with pop idol/actor/entrepreneur Adam Faith. He makes a point of introducing him to me when he drops in at the office. I can still feel the grip of Adam's hand as he reaches towards me with a radiant smile. He is wearing Cuban heeled boots and is shorter than I expected, but much more dynamic.

The Beatles have become too famous to wander into the office. A year or so earlier John Lennon had sat on journalists' desks irreverently and cracked jokes. He even agreed to be photographed leaping up and down on a bomb site. The Stones are not yet unreachable. It is possible to chat to them on the phone at their manager Andrew Oldham's office. The magazine runs a ghosted column featuring a different Stone each week. We take turns at writing it. I remember Mick Jagger's bored voice at the end of the line when I tried pumping him for news for his spot.

"What you been doing Mick?"

"Having a ball. *Screwing* all the birds!" I have no reason to doubt it. My mind has gone blank and can't I think of any more questions.

One of the first groups I interview are the Moody Blues. They come to the office an *Undiscovered British Group*. Every week the magazine features an *Undiscovered British Group*. They mostly stay undiscovered.

The Moodies come carrying the obligatory stage suits for the photo session, in plastic bags with zips. They have all been leaders of different groups in Birmingham. Mike Pinder, the keyboard player, hands me a demo of *Go Now*. He explains that it started to climb the charts but has dropped. I play the emotional single on my record player until it wears thin. My write-up starts a ripple of interest and soon *Go Now* begins to climb the charts again to Number One, earning the Moodies a silver disc.

Less than a month after I join the magazine, I am sent to Paris for three days with the Animals who are making a documentary for French TV. Their recording of *House of the Rising Sun* is Number One in the charts in the UK, France, and America. They take me to the trendiest nightclubs and dose me with champagne and brandy. I am impressed by their intelligence and humility. Everywhere we go in this romantic city, the first ever folk-rock hit *House of the Rising Sun,* is being played.

Fragment Two: A Bedsit In Hampstead

TONY is unconventional and beautiful. He towers over me. Once he slapped me round the face so hard I nearly fell over. I have discovered his unpredictable outbursts are part of the package. I had been waiting for him for what seemed an eternity. Then he suddenly appeared on a Hampstead street one spring evening. I had been gate-crashing parties. I loved him immediately.

I went back with him to his bedsit, early in the morning, after we had invaded more parties and stopped at a coffee stall on a bridge high over the Thames. I remember staring down into the dark, shimmering river. I had known him only a few hours. I stayed with him because I was afraid of losing him.

We spend a restless night on a single bed in an attic, hardly big enough for someone half Tony's size. He must have rented this place in desperation or because he wanted unconsciously to squeeze back inside the womb. He refuses to kiss me, and I refuse to make love. I lay beside him in a navy-blue lace slip, alarmed when I hear him grinding his teeth in his sleep.

Next morning we go to a workman's caff for a fry-up. It is unusually hot and sunny for early May. I feel deliriously happy walking beside him along the elegant avenues of Hampstead. Clusters of white flowers are erect on the shady horse chestnuts. Whenever I gaze into his gorgeous face my heart goes into spasms of joy. He is so attractive and he is beside me. I am floating, not walking.

He has arranged to meet someone, so we separate. I feel anxious. Maybe I won't see him again? There is a strong possibility he will forget me as quickly as yesterday. I drive home along the North Circular Road like someone who has just woken from a trance.

Nine months later I feel an entirely different person. It is as if a third being exists, has come to dwell between us, somehow entered in, part of both of us and never content unless we are together. This new, third being now dominates everything.

The Puritanism of earlier decades still hangs in the air. There was no sex education at school. Sister Mary Stephen, the headmistress, warned us not to hold hands with boys because it "aroused the passions". In biology classes we studied the life cycle of the frog. Some of the girls who were more advanced and less studious already had boyfriends, picked up from the nearby public school on the way home. They indulged in more interesting experiments than those conducted in the science lab.

I remember sitting in a classroom with the lid of my desk propped up devouring the first page of a paperback my best friend had shoved into my hands at break. I sensed the steely eyes of Sister Mary Ingrid penetrating the cover. I had only had time to read a few paragraphs of *Tom Boy*. The heroine is wrestling in jeans, naked to the waist. Her opponent, a young guy, grabs her breasts.

"Where did you get THIS?" Sister Ingrid demanded icily, examining the contents through traumatised spectacles.

"Pauline gave it...."

Looking back, I am appalled by my fear and betrayal of my best friend.

"Where did you get THIS, Pauline?"

"Someone left it on the train, Sister." The shocking paperback is sent to Sister Mary Stephen, the headmistress.

Sister Mary Stephen is convinced that Pauline with her immaculate school uniform and enviable shoulder-length, ash blonde hair, is an innocent victim. After all, the school motto is *Veritas* - Latin for truth - and she is a prefect, has the looks of an angel. But she had been tempted on her way to school, at the newsagents on the corner. She had bought the explicit book along with a bar of Cadbury's strawberry cream chocolate.

The nuns conclude that an evil man, bent on corrupting young minds, had deliberately left the book on the train. It is confiscated.

My parents hadn't been particularly helpful about sex. After my periods started they gave me a booklet to read with clinical diagrams of the womb, ovaries, and vagina, misleadingly called *The Facts of Life*.

Maggie, one of my school friends, planned to be pregnant all the time when she grew up so that she wouldn't have to endure period pains. I remembered when I was a little girl seeing buckets of blood being carried down from the bedroom after my mother miscarried. Once I was caught sitting on the stairs with my brother, blowing up condoms into magnificent white balloons.

Tony's room is at the top of a Regency house in a warren of bedsitters where unseen people exist in the form of footsteps, creaks, muffled voices. Here, and in many other similar rooms, for he changes residence frequently and unpredictably, I have rid myself of my inhibitions and been initiated into what surprisingly has become a spiritual journey.

I have been cosmically tuned, liberated from my body as Tony's body becomes part of my own.

Where I am heading is uncertain. Tony has no plans at all, only to meet me after I finish work. He is an unemployed actor recovering from a breakdown. He lives from hand to mouth, asking strangers for money in his lovely theatrical voice. I never dwell upon his insecurity or try to persuade him to get a job. We rely upon the only stability we know, in each other's arms.

The first Christmas after we meet Tony is too poor to buy presents. He has been invited to my home but feels uncomfortable about having nothing to give.

"It doesn't matter. Just come. My parents aren't expecting you to bring anything!"

My father is a materialist. He believes his pocket is his best friend and has unsuccessfully tried to instil this belief into me. He is at a loss to understand why I am dating a penniless guy who wears tight jeans, ripped t-shirts, and is emotionally unstable. He once met Tony in the street, on his way to the house. He told him he thought he was unsuitable for me. Neither of us took any notice.

At first I am delighted when Tony unravels the print of Gaugin's boldly coloured painting *Who Are We? Where Do We Come From? Where Are We Going?* It will remind me of him each time I gaze at it. Then he rips it up, destroying the whole of Christmas in a split second. Why? He simply can't handle my fierce reaction when I discover that earlier he had bumped into Mick Jagger in the street in Chelsea. He had cycled over there on an old bike he found dumped by some railings. He had asked Mick for a hand-out, telling him *I* worked on ***Boyfriend*** and was ***his*** girlfriend. Mick had responded generously. But I now feel humiliated that Mick Jagger has paid for my Christmas present!

Afterwards, I tape the torn masterpiece together with tears in my eyes. Months later I still have the mutilated print on my bedroom wall. It is one of the few material things Tony has given me - or was it really from Mick Jagger? But the fact that he has actually touched it makes it incredibly special. How silly love is, and how fragile.

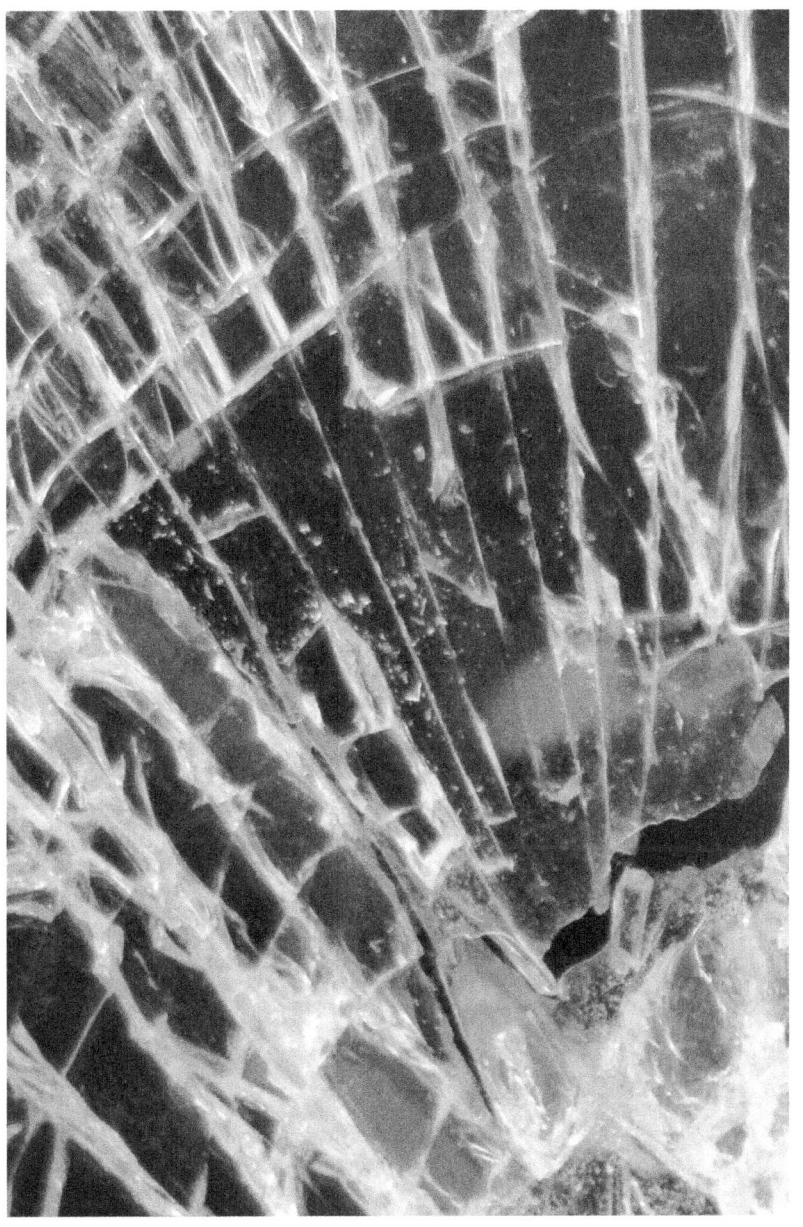

Fragment Three: Old-Fashioned Waiters Serving Champagne

THE man sitting beside me on a stall in a Soho coffee bar is wearing an expensive overcoat and a muffler. He is Kit Lambert, son of Constant Lambert the composer. He is well-bred and finely educated - a most unlikely person to be joint manager of the Who.

It is a freezing afternoon in late November. I have been working on the magazine for a just a few weeks when he phones hoping for some publicity. He is grateful that I have agreed to accept his invitation to coffee. He is carrying a briefcase and is extremely intense.

He explains that he has taken on an unknown West London group, the High Numbers, after combing the clubs for talent. They have been renamed the Who. When I discover his business partner is Chris Stamp, brother of Terence Stamp the actor, we are suddenly on common ground. I have met Chris because he is a close friend of my brother who is an actor. When Kit phoned my office he had no idea of the connection. He is thrilled.

Kit and Chris worked together as assistant film directors. Kit explains that they have decided to take on a pop group as a way of financing their own movies. Chris, from the East End, can see the potential of the Who for appealing to Mods like themselves, kids who are underprivileged, frustrated, and take speed to liven things up.

On this cold afternoon, as we discuss the possibility for a little publicity, neither Kit nor I have an inkling of the legend the Who will become.

Kit hands me a demo of *I Can't Explain*, their first single. I imagine it's about a kid who gets high on drugs. Later Pete Townshend tells me it's a love song. Not long after this auspicious meeting I receive an invitation to a reception for the Who in Belgravia. It is held in a luxurious flat that Kit and Chris are renting and is attended by the London Press. *I Can't Explain* is played repeatedly and old-fashioned waiters in black suits and bow ties, who look as if they have been borrowed specially for the occasion from a banquet at Buckingham Palace, offer us champagne on silver trays.

The Who are wandering around sticking out like sore thumbs in this sophisticated setting. Chris and Kit are in fact so broke at this point that they are expecting to be evicted by bailiffs!

I can never forget how Kit ushered me into his bedroom to show me the cutting from the magazine pinned on the wall. It is the first publicity the group has received, and he is delighted with the few paragraphs I have managed to squeeze in.

Accompanied by a rabble of gate-crashing friends, I leave after a couple of hours, tipsy with champagne and elated as we float down flights of plush carpet to the strains of *I Can't Explain.*

Over the coming months the Who begin to have a huge influence on the pop scene, using gimmicks that make them stand out. I interview them at my office on a number of occasions, fascinated to see how they are evolving.

By April they are performing at the Marquee Club in Wardour Street and Pete has started smashing electric guitars. I write:

'*Pete Townshend - tall, thin, long, spiky, expressive hands, a red spotlight shining on him in the darker than half-light - crashes across the strings of a guitar, twists the amplifiers so that the feed-back keeps coming through and he brutally bangs his guitar forward. There is stiffness and abandon. What is happening?*

Drummer, Keith Moon, dark fringe falling into his eyes, the hair separated with perspiration. Almost maniacal, rolling his drumsticks, going wild, opening his mouth, closing his eyes.

Bass guitarist John Entwistle stands tall and sinister, unmoved by the movement around him. He stands looking powerful and strong.

Roger Daltry, singer, wields and pulls at the microphone, almost performing to it alone. Wriggling and reeling, singing words you can't hear, frighteningly.

The Who gathered round and straight-talked.

"We hate weak sounds like many of the groups have."

They look surprisingly harmless after their gyrations on stage.'

Later, I write that Keith, has a loudspeaker in every room in his home so that there is perpetual sound. He looks so innocent. He blinks his huge brown eyes and buries himself still blinking playfully behind a newspaper during an interview at my office. It is difficult to imagine at this point that he will die in a hotel room, a victim of his excesses.

Roger tells me, *"I was once, a not very good guitarist in a group."* Most talkative is Pete. He sidles in and out of the doorway of the office as he chats, wearing a jazzy blue shirt and light cotton jacket.

"I started making the strange sound effects first by mainly having the amplifiers too loud. Now it's used to push over ideas we can't get across any other way. We think this is the true way of playing a guitar. By banging the speakers with the guitar I can get certain unique effects."

Fans tattoo themselves with their name, or a small arrow, to demonstrate their affection for the group.'

By July 3, 1965 I am writing that the Who play pop art music because their sounds are not purely musical but full of the noise of the streets and lives around them. They are also designing and making up their own clothes, wearing original, pop art gear. John has a jacket made out of a Union Jack. Keith's white polo-neck sweater with a target on the front was inspired by the wing of a jet plane. Roger wears a leather belt decorated with insulating tape.

Pete is considered the intellectual of the group. He is unafraid to speak his mind and loves to be outrageously extravagant. He discards new clothes three weeks after he buys them. And he insists on having the most expensive guitars although they end up being smashed against his amplifier. He feels that if he used a cheap, crummy guitar it would be insincere.

By December the Who are promoting their latest song, *My Generation.*

"No, there's no message in this number," Pete assures me. *"It's a song about feelings. I Can't Explain was a song about love. Anyway, Anyhow, Anywhere was about a young bloke who was cocky and thought he could do anything he wanted.*

My Generation, I suppose is a slightly nostalgic song. It reminds us of the days before the Mod thing started dwindling, the time when there was a feeling in the air that you could run down the streets without any responsibilities, and get stoned out of your mind and smash windows. You see the Mods are getting older. I'm twenty now and most of the fellas who were in my year at school have stopped being Mods and have joined the army or got jobs in factories and stuff like that.

The stammering on the record is a way of demonstrating the inability of young people to express themselves. "

Fragment Four: Smashed Windows

TONY has a need to smash windows. He has put his fist through countless panes of glass. It seems that the impact somehow brings him in touch with reality. Once he smashed a Pyrex coffee cup when he was sitting with me outside a café in Hampstead. The coffee poured down my legs and over my feet, soaked into the pavement.

I was so in love with him right from the beginning that any kind of anti-social behaviour would have made no difference to my feelings. I feel a kind of worship for him. It comes welling up inside me like sunshine. Everything he touches or possesses is charmed. He possesses so little – a few pairs of boots; shirts he never wears, on wire hangers; numerous ties; paperback books; a chest expander. His body is attractively toned.

Leslie Bainbridge, editor of *Health and Efficiency*, which is produced in an office above mine, seems to have gone to extremes with what he refers to as *the body beautiful*. He appears to be bursting out of his shirt. But he is undeniably a brilliant advertisement for his naturist magazine, with his bulging muscles, clear, amused eyes and toothpaste smile. His dark hair is combed back from his forehead. He could double for Tarzan. He is polite and well-spoken and surprisingly shy, despite the fact that he spends his weekends at naturist camps and plays tennis in the nude.

My mother sees him on television in a programme about naturism. He is being interviewed naked, cooking sausages over a primer stove. I like him. I go up to his office for chats while he is having Ryvita and a banana for his lunch.

"*The body beautiful*," he says, drinking in his words like most people inhale cigarette smoke. "*The body beautiful* has always been my aim."

He takes from his drawer photographs of himself entering the Mr Universe contest. When he feels daring he slips me pictures with naked girls poised on each of his shoulders.

He abhors bad language. "Anglo-Saxon is for love-making," he says. But I find it hard to imagine him being anything but polite, even in bed.

Ken has the job of writing verse to go underneath the naked women who are featured in *Health and Efficiency*. They are photographed pushing lawn mowers and performing other equally bizarre tasks, with the naughty bits masked out.

When Tony is suffering from a bout of psychosis Leslie volunteers to stay at our house and protect us while my father is away on business. Despite his powerful body he is the most gentle of men. He sits on the single bed in the guest room waiting patiently to be called down to breakfast.

After Leslie's visit my mother buys a juice extractor because she is so impressed with how fit he looks on fresh orange juice.

Fortunately, Tony didn't come round to the house that evening and cause any trouble. But a few days earlier, when my mother bolted the door on him, he climbed over the garden wall and forced his way in. He was desperate to speak to me. He can't tolerate any form of rejection.

When we first met he wasn't so vulnerable. As time passes I become a symbol of stability. In the early days he is able to be aloof and distant without much effort, because I am new in a life filled with trauma from which he will never recover.

A student called Liz, tried to kill herself because he rejected her. She reacted by bursting into the room next to his and jumping out of the sixth-floor window.

"This is goodbye!" she shouted dramatically. She landed in a rosebush and miraculously only broke her leg.

Tony, who attracts women easily with his stunning looks, had told her he wasn't in love with her, although he had slept with her. She is an Oxford undergraduate. He explained he was attracted to her mind.

When I meet Liz her leg is in plaster and she is limping. Tony feels guilty. I am glad she is plain but wary of her intelligence, and beautifully manicured nails which Tony also admires. My hands are strong and practical, and I find it hard to grow my nails. Yet he somehow becomes addicted to me. He says my skin smells of freshly sharpened pencils.

For a while I resist him. Eventually he announces sullenly, "Don't you know you are making me ill?"

One warm evening, I finally give in and Tony is stunned. For several confused weeks he has tried to gently break down my resistance. So he feels he owns me now, that's why he is so jealous and creates scenes.

We don't socialise much. Whenever we do it usually ends in disaster. Tony takes me to a party and after we arrive, disappears. Next day he phones begging to see me.

His unpredictable behaviour makes me unpredictable. I am good at paying him back. He asks me to drive him to the cigarette machine in Belsize Village. He leaves his room with bare feet. I deliberately drive off while he is dropping coins into the slot. He walks home over the cold pavements, smoking.

The Moody Blues have become internationally successful. They throw a party at their new home, a mansion by the Thames. Sandie Shaw, Lulu and Ray Davies are on the glittering guest list along with all sorts of celebrities. Graeme Edge, the Moodies' drummer, greets me with an enormous hug. But Tony takes this completely the wrong way.

"Get your hands OFF her!" he orders. I die of embarrassment.

Later when I apologise, Graeme is endearingly laid back about Tony's paranoia.

"He must love you a hell of a lot," he says kindly.

Mike McGrath, publicist for John Stephen the creator of Carnaby Street, then arrives with the worst possible timing. He is a really flamboyant gay who never utters a word without simultaneously touching you. He draws me into a potentially lethal conversation as I stand with my back against a wall, trying hard to keep my distance.

I decide to leave before Tony totally freaks out.

Fragment Five: A Dutch Cap

MY fear of getting pregnant appears to have acted as a brake. What on earth would I have done with a baby? Now I see this isn't so. What has protected me is lack of temptation. I have been seeking my own flesh or something as near to it as possible. Now I want Tony's body to be MY body, to turn myself inside out and consume him.

I am naive in many ways. I am also a rebel, hate to conform for the sake of conforming. But I use my head, see consequences and try, if sometimes half-heartedly, to avoid them.

I decide to sleep with Tony quite deliberately, at the moment I choose. My decisions always depend on how I feel. Feelings dominate. I try my hardest never to do anything I do not feel right about. It isn't always easy. There are pressures from everywhere, especially from those who have already sold out and done what is easiest and most practical.

I am determined to sing my own song, even if it is obviously and horribly out of tune. But being an unmarried mother is not an attractive proposition in the Sixties and socially unacceptable. Adoption or abortion is the usual method of dealing with unwanted babies. Others get married.

Maddy, a close, college friend, offers her contraceptive pills. They are the latest thing and creating a sexual revolution. They upset my delicate hormonal balance and make me nauseous.

Condoms can only be purchased furtively at chemists, and there is a device known as a Dutch cap, made of rubber, and worn internally. It must be fitted by a doctor and used with spermicide cream that attacks potential babies. Maddy knows a private doctor in

Kingston. I see her twice at great expense, firstly to be measured and then to have the cap fitted.

The cap, supposed to be less restrictive than a condom during sex, turns out to be uncomfortable and messy. The spermicide takes hours to work and the cap doesn't stay in place. After a few attempts I decide I am more likely to get pregnant if I use it. We decide to be old-fashioned and try condoms.

Gradually, as we become more and more intimate, I learn about Tony's past. He lived with a girl called Ann and had two children with her. She was older than Tony and wanted to marry him. He wasn't ready, so she married someone else.

Tony doesn't seem concerned about his children. He has left them behind like discarded newspapers on a train. But as time passes he starts fantasising about the children he and I will have, and dreams up unusual names for them.

One of my friends gets herself pregnant deliberately. I meet her on the street by chance. She looks pale and a bump is protruding through her loose clothes. Her boyfriend comes from a wealthy family. Months later she is seen at a tea party, breast feeding as serenely as the Madonna, and proudly wearing a wedding ring.

Another friend, Jenny a vicar's daughter, made love to a Spanish Gypsy in Ibiza when she was sixteen and became pregnant. Her parents sent her to stay with an aunt. She sang hymns in a cubicle in the maternity ward to comfort herself during labour. The baby was whisked away and adopted before she had even finished singing.

Kate has had a number of abortions. I sit with her all night after one of these expensive, private operations. Her cheeks turn the colour of wax. Her boyfriend is a swine and quite

24

unworthy of her. I am more interested in my career than having babies. Babies are something in the distant future. I have no desire to get pregnant but cease to be afraid of the possibility. I will deal with it should it happen.

The assistant photographer on the magazine is called Vic. He is 18, and half Italian. He comes from Balham in South London and is sunny and enthusiastic. The main part of his job is developing films. He glows in the dark room in his white coat. Sometimes he is sent out on jobs with me to gain work experience. Vic says exactly what he thinks and tends to put his foot in it. He accompanies me to interview Marianne Faithfull. She is still in her teens and married to a successful young businessman. Her affair with Mick Jagger and attempted suicide are still ahead.

"When you come up go straight into the lounge. I'm feeding the baby." Marianne's voice flows mellifluously through the intercom outside the front door of a house in Knightsbridge. She lives in a luxurious flat on the third floor. She appears in a long, green, quilted housecoat. She resembles a Hans Christian Andersen princess.

"I'm sorry to keep you waiting but the baby's feeding times have got mixed up and I've changed the routine."

"How do you feel about being a mother?" I ask. "You said after the birth that it had given you a new dimension."

"It is difficult to describe the difference. But I do realise he has nobody else in the world. He is completely dependent on me, especially as I'm feeding him myself."

I ask if she is bringing up Nicholas in any particular way." I'll just let him happen. I haven't any theories."

Vic is obviously embarrassed by Marianne's reference to breast feeding. Afterwards I assure him that it is perfectly natural.

Vic lands me in awkward situations but nevertheless amuses me. At Elstree Studios the electricians threaten to go on strike when Vic messes around with the lighting. He is photographing Dudley Moore who is shooting a comedy with Peter Cooke called *Thirty Is A Dangerous Age Cynthia*. Peter sits in a director's chair with his name on, reading *The Times* and ignoring us.

We need a glamour pic of Dudley, who unlike Peter has become somewhat of a heartthrob. Vic asks him to poke his head through the rungs of a ladder and gives him a mop and bucket to hold. Dudley goes along with this with a mischievous little smile on his face. The ladder shot is a favourite with the magazine's chief photographer when posing groups. Vic imitates what he believes is supreme professionalism.

On another occasion we interview drummer Dave Clark, of the Dave Clark Five. Good-looking Dave lives in a posh property aptly named *The Drum*. Afterwards returning to the office in a minicab, which Dave has kindly summoned, Vic comments on how charming he is, and adds that he has heard rumours that he is gay.

Back at my desk I receive a phone call from Dave's publicist.

"You know why I'm calling Christine, don't you?"

I am mystified.

Apparently the minicab driver has gone straight back to Dave's home and repeated our conversation in a somewhat distorted fashion. I manage to defuse the situation by explaining that Vic had only *repeated* what he had *heard*.

Vic is mortified and decides to return to *The Drum* and apologise personally for any misunderstanding. But when he arrives by bus, Dave is away and his dad answers the door.

The saddest thing is when Vic suddenly develops multiple sclerosis and is no longer able to work. One day he collapses in the street at Tooting Bec and a Black guy carries him home in his arms like a child.

Fragment Six: A Sports Car

I accompany Clive, my brother, to one of his psychoanalytical sessions in Hove. The distance from the London suburbs is fifty miles. We travel in his brand-new sports car, a white Austin Healey Sprite. I have total trust in him, am oblivious of his James Dean driving. I am full of admiration when we come to a traffic jam and he pulls on to the verge and skims past the waiting cars.

He falls in love with the beautiful contours of the South Downs as we approach the Sussex coast. It is Christmas Eve. After his session with Mr Barker in a Regency house in Brunswick Square, Clive does all his Christmas shopping at *Hills of Hove*, the bustling department store on the Western Road. Coffee bars are crowded with trendy young people wearing expensive clothes.

Mr Barker retired from being a Methodist minister and trained as a psychotherapist after developing a tumour on his vocal cords. He lost the use of his voice following an operation and now speaks on his breath, in a hushed whisper. He believes his ill-health was psychosomatic and stemmed from unhappiness and frustration. The tightness in his throat started as a child. Self-expression was thwarted by his strict upbringing and he was not supposed to cry.

"When a baby is stifled and not nurtured, cracks begin to show later in life in challenging situations, because the vulnerable baby hiding behind the mask of maturity cannot cope," Mr Barker explains. His work involves nurturing and encouraging this baby self and allowing his clients free expression without fear. He tells my parents that although Clive has been ill it is possible to help him. He diagnoses him as schizoid. Part of him has split off to survive emotionally, but he is not fragmented as is the case in schizophrenia.

Clive has always been different, ahead of his time. He is gifted at getting attention, particularly from women. He makes them feel special. This includes my mother. I hero-worship him. He was mean to me until I was sixteen but after that we had developed a deep friendship. He takes me for my first Chinese meal at the Hong Kong Emporium at Leicester Square. He is studying at RADA and meets me outside the tube wearing jeans, a long black jumper - and sunglasses, because it's cool.

Strangely, despite the excruciating breakdown he is soon to experience, it is only Clive, out of the all the family, to whom I can really relate.

When he is eighteen Clive lost his temper with my father and banged his fist down with such force on the table at breakfast that he smashed all the crockery. My father has been lecturing him about spending the weekend with his fiancé, actress Christine Collins, at her home in the country. He thinks he is too young to get serious and should be concentrating on his acting career.

Clive likes to shock, use everyday life as his stage. There are always arguments going on in the house. I see marriage as a terrible kind of imprisonment.

"You have to change yourself if you want to change your life. It requires a complete revolution. It is pointless trying to change another person," says Mr Barker. As far back as I can remember Clive has always been acting. When he was eight, he had a metal box full of professional greasepaints, also black fluffy stuff to make beards, moustaches or sideburns. He and a friend dressed up as old tramps and staggered along the street with walking sticks.

Once they converted the garden shed into *The Chamber of Horrors*. I had to be the corpse covered in an old sheet, a noose around my neck. We charged other children a penny entrance fee. One little girl burst into tears and ran away after Clive forced her to touch my shrouded head and told her the hair underneath was matted with dried blood!

Clive played a girl with plaits in Emlyn William's play *Dear Evelyn* when he appeared with the Redcliff Players at a hall in Earls Court. My father was in charge of special effects backstage, bending sheets of flimsy metal to make impressive claps of thunder.

I told everyone I met in the ladies' cloakroom in the interval, "*Caroline is not really a girl. She is my brother wearing a wig.*" I can't keep secrets.

Fragment Seven: Ripped T-Shirts

TONY walked off the stage at the Mermaid Theatre in the middle of a performance. His career has been entirely theatrical. He slept with a director to get himself into rep. He is quite open about the fact. There was no other way.

He attracts the attention of some wealthy gays who live in luxurious properties in Hampstead at the top of Haverstock Hill. Tony and I sometimes run into them on our way down from Hampstead Station to his room. He camps it up for their benefit.

I wonder if an experience with a man in his past has given him an identity crisis. Sometimes he acts strangely in front of my father. Once he pranced around the living room on tiptoe. When he isn't well Tony becomes more effeminate.

He was in rep at Edinburgh and also worked with the Young Vic Company. Amazingly he can recite *The Complete Works of Shakespeare* from memory.

Sometimes he meets me wearing a t-shirt ripped across the front and torn jeans. His feet are bare and he has leather thong knotted around his wrists. For 1965 this is incredibly way-out. He somehow manages to look gorgeous. All his underwear is pale pink because the colours ran in a washing machine in the laundrette.

I accept him totally as he is. I love him more with each passing moment. He needs to be noticed, parading around Hampstead, seeming to exist on a higher level.

He hasn't worked as an actor for some time. I can't remember ever discussing with him whether or not he wants to return to the theatre. He talks of travelling, writing books, but doesn't really have any plans, just to be with me.

He works for a scaffolding company for a while when we first meet. He gets up at the crack of dawn to go to building sites.

He behaves quite normally for periods and I am happy. Then suddenly, for no apparent reason, he doesn't want to see me and stays endlessly in bed. He talks about having had treatment at a hospital in Epsom but he is terrified now of doctors, of being confined and sedated.

When he has nowhere else to go he stays in a basement flat that belongs to an old lady who is in hospital. She keeps stray cats and there is an overpowering stench. Tony's face is covered in perspiration and he is delusional. He tells me, *"Go. GET OUT!"* He can't handle any kind of communication or closeness.

Soon he is on the phone, pleading to see me.

Sometimes he slaps my face really hard. Usually this comes out of the blue, because he has misinterpreted something I've said. He doesn't batter me or anything as awful as that. Surprisingly, he doesn't even bruise me. He simply lashes out and then bitterly regrets it.

I am trying to handle his mood swings and at the same time meeting musicians who are destined to become icons, famous throughout the world because of their music. I know them before they make their major breakthrough and help with my interviews to manipulate their destinies.

In March, Tom Jones appears in my office. Any recording artist who gets into the Top Twenty, automatically qualifies for an interview. They all have PROs eagerly seeking publicity on their behalf.

It's Not Unusual has soared to Number One and Tom, from near Cardiff, is remarkably unassuming. His interview with me is his first in London. I have been working on the magazine for about four months. My interviewing techniques have improved. I am more confident.

Tom is dressed in black trousers, a denim shirt, black tie and short overcoat with a velvet collar. He wears the same fashionable Chelsea boots as the Beatles. Around his wrist is a silver identity bracelet.

Vic captures him forever, looking pensive and moody on an ornate bench in a nearby, elegant square.

"When I go home and visit the local my old mates, instead of slapping me on the back and yelling to the barman - 'Hey get Tommy a drink!' - don't act so friendly anymore 'cos they're afraid I'll think they're trying to get around me now I've made a name for myself," he explains. Tall and tapered, broad-shouldered and strong. On stage he's hard and sexy. In real life he's the type of man who bottles up his feelings for just so long and then whoosh! – it all comes out like a clap of thunder. Then things start happening – or they used to – like getting into punch-ups and having his nose knocked out of shape.'

Later Tom has cosmetic surgery on his broken nose, just like Maddy my girlfriend, who gets a nose job on the National Health and goes retroussé.

Tom tells me he had singing lessons with a prima donna.

"You're wasting your time boy going on the pop scene,' she said. 'Become an opera singer."

Outrageous American singer PJ Proby rents a four-storey house in Chelsea.

"'No!" he was shouting down the phone when I arrive to interview him. "I don't go back to the States till I go as big as the Beatles!"

His long hair, wet from shampooing, dangles on his shoulders. One of two attractive girls serves me an iced drink. A guy brings out a shiny metal hair dryer and begins curling PJ's hair round a brush. He lets it fall softly on his shoulders.

He is wearing buckled shoes and a navy-blue parachuting suit. He reclines on a low sofa and I ask him what influences he has had on the British pop scene.

"I've brought colour. There's no one as colourful as me. Well, is there?"

All the cabbies in London know him and the off-licence across the street gets regular orders for crates of beer and large cigars.'

His grandiose thinking is highly contagious. When I leave, I feel I can achieve *anything.*

Years later I meet the Sixties legend when he has survived a total media ban, bankruptcy, and alcoholism. He is stone-cold sober and sipping mineral water.

His dream was to be a movie star and he sang on demos that Elvis recorded. In 1964 he appeared with the Beatles on British television and cut a series of singles including *Hold Me* and *Somewhere.* But while on tour with Cilla Black, his velvet trousers split at Castle Hall, Croydon on January 29, 1965. They split again at the Ritz Cinema, London on January 31. He was pulled off the tour and replaced by Tom Jones.

Proby's raunchy act deeply offended the show business hierarchy. He was subsequently barred from every major theatre in Britain and from the TV network.

'"I gave the audience at the Royal Albert Hall a James Brown act, moving in the style of Black singers. They had never seen anything like it. My ponytail wasn't real. It was bobby pinned so hard that trickles of blood ran down my neck," he recalls.

"I was furious that night because my swashbuckling shirt hadn't turned up. To teach my manager a lesson I got a friend to rip open the seams of my t-shirt and then tack them back together. I came bounding on to Turn On Your Love Light. The t-shirt disintegrated.

The audience rushed the stage and seats got ripped out. The split t-shirt was my only stunt. I didn't do it to become a sex symbol, but to show my manager. The pants didn't split that time.

After that I was allowed to have loads of velvet costumes. I had them made to form fit. There was no such thing as stretch velvet in 1965. The reason they split was that my act was so physical. But they only split at the knees and a little up the side of the leg.

Flesh had never been shown in England. Then, when all seven of my suits split while I was on tour, I was told: 'Change your clothes or you'll be thrown off.' I ignored it. My critics thought if I had no place to work I would leave the country."'

Fragment Eight: A Flying Bread Roll

I celebrated my 21st birthday with a meal for four in a bistro in the King's Road.

My father refused to come. He bases his decision on the fact that I had been living away from home. He obviously doesn't approve of me trying to be independent. I'd been sharing a flat in Warwick Avenue, near Maida Vale, with Christine Collins, now Clive's ex-fiancé. It hasn't worked out particularly well. I've had difficulty meeting my share of the bills.

The flat was on the second floor of an Edwardian house and the entrance hall always smelt of curry. My room looked out on to ugly backyards. I painted it tangerine and pink, and bought a kitten at a pet shop. The kitten hated being cooped up inside and grew wilder every day.

Christine disliked Tony. She disliked him more when he smashed a pane of glass in the front door when I refused to let him in. Christine was half his size but flew at him with her claws out.

Tony cut his hand trying to make the door safe and afterwards went to the hospital to have the gash stitched.

I was glad when Christine went into rep for a while. I used her room, which was more comfortable and had a rented telly. But there was a terrible row when Christine came back unexpectedly and found me in there entertaining friends. Looking back, I don't blame her.

Tony called a taxi and helped me move my things. He found a new room with French windows in a rundown square in Hampstead. He borrowed a couple of coffee mugs and bought a tin of food for the kitten. He went to a lot of trouble really. But he became irate because I felt this room was the end of the line. I should have been more tactful. He saw it as the beginning of sharing our lives. I wondered where we would go from here, sharing a bathroom with strangers and cooking on a gas ring?

He lashed out and I ran away out into the dark with the black kitten in my arms. The following evening my mother drove over to collect my things.

I go back home but only manage to keep away from Tony's lonely room for a couple of days. He sends me a valentine card with *Je t'aime* inscribed in pink plastic roses, and for my birthday a Françoise Sagan novel, *A Certain Smile*. Inside he writes *I Love You* on different pages in English and in French.

My colleagues buy me a pale blue shortie nightie with two layers of nylon as fine as butterfly wings. Kate gives me a mini handbag made of black patent leather, shaped like a doctor's bag. My mother pays for me to have a ring created at an exclusive jewellers in Mayfair, a huge chunk of amethyst, my birthstone, set in claws of gold.

During my birthday celebrations Mick Jagger and his girlfriend Chrissy Shrimpton - sister of super model Jean, and secretary to Andrew Oldham the Stones' Manager - are sitting at the next table quietly chatting. Chrissy is extremely pretty, with short blonde hair. They are literary inches away from us.

My mother's bread roll flies on to Mick's table as she attempts to cut it. Mick grins and passes it back. *Mick seems to be haunting me.*

Clive is with his new girlfriend Fran and pays for the meal. They are sharing a flat in Sloane Street and eat out in King's Road every evening. Clive knows people and gets special deals.

Fragment Nine: A Silver Bird

CLIVE is over that awful period when he returns home and spends most of his time in bed. He is deeply in love with Fran who has the huge brown eyes and full lips of an Italian actress. She works at the pirate radio station *Radio Caroline*.

When Clive brings her home she wears my clothes without asking. When I protest she pouts like a spoilt child. Clive takes her fishing at the Grand Union Canal, just a short walk away along a footpath lined with factories. She changes into my denim skirt.

Not that it's unusual to swop clothes. I wear Clive's tight Levi's when I am slim enough to squeeze into them and pull up the zip. I borrow his pale blue, V-neck sweater and he warns me not to leave *breast marks*. I also fit into his long, soft black leather boots which he had specially made by Covent Garden footwear company *Anello & Davide.*

Levi's are a religion. I remember going to Cadogan Gardens in Chelsea where Clive was sharing a penthouse with Chris Stamp, before he went into the pop business. I was eighteen and working at the Weekly Post in Ickenham, as a trainee reporter.

Chris and Clive lived on fresh fruit salad and visited health farms with a view to getting as slim as possible so that their jeans fitted like second skins around their bums. I remember Clive opening the door in a pair of wet Levi's he had been shrinking in the bath.

Clive has appeared in a black and white movie with Terry Stamp, who spotted him acting on TV. Terry asked his agent to contact Clive because he thought he had talent. The movie, *Term of Trial,* also starred Sir Lawrence Olivier, Simone Signoret, and Sarah Miles.

Later Terry introduced Clive to his brother Chris, and they have become close friends.

When they are broke Clive and Chris rent a room in Ladbroke Grove - in those days an extremely seedy area. I go to visit Clive by tube, lugging carrier bags full of groceries donated by my mother. Sometimes he summons me to gloomy bedsitters for no apparent reason. I realise he is scared of being on his own because sometimes he loses his identity.

Because I love him with the same depth and admiration that I love Tony, I am easy to manipulate. I am afraid for both, but neither of them is afraid for me. The dangerous time begins when Clive grows interested in drugs. At first it is all a fantasy. Because he is an actor he tends to read about people in books and then live the part.

He reads a book called *Viper: Confessions of A Drug Addict* by Raymond Thorp. Junkies in the early Sixties are a rarity. Clive is fascinated by them. He takes me to *Boots'* late-night pharmacy at Piccadilly to observe junkies turning up for their prescriptions.

One afternoon we roll up Typhoo tea in cigarette papers and pretend to get high.

The first time I smoke pot is at a girlfriend's flat in Hampstead. I take a few puffs from a joint, holding the smoke inside my lungs as instructed. Later I drive down Haverstock Hill in my two-tone Hillman California with red leather seats. I am stunned by the magical glow of the traffic lights - red, amber, and green, in the luminous early evening with a crescent moon in the sky.

Marijuana and hashish gently filter into my life and those of my friends. I go to a party where a guy with long hair passes round a hubble-bubble as if he were serving Holy Communion.

There is a sudden and definite change in outlook and perception. Why has everyone stopped experiencing the world we live in fully? Why are the tulips on the softly flowing dining room curtains so beautiful? Why does Clive laugh when I exclaim, "Wow!" Why have they - we - never been happy until this moment? Why has everything been so dismal, so difficult, grey?

Nearly everyone I know starts getting in touch with their senses, their taste buds, particularly in kitchens at parties, in Indian restaurants. Nearly everyone I know is getting in touch with their bodies. Kisses in dark corners become eternal. Love filters in with the psychedelic music. Worship of colour. We are grown-up children in an earthly paradise. We stop drinking beer and wine at parties and smoke pot instead. Smoking offers a much deeper and more pleasurable experience. Alcohol tends to blot out everything and then you're sick in someone's front garden.

The best thing is how we sit round and roll up joints and share our thoughts. We really *listen* to music because for the first time we *hear* it. We appear to become more gentle and mystical.

The Fuzz haven't caught on yet. We smoke joints on the train from Wembley Park to Baker Street and nobody sitting reading a newspaper recognises the enticing aroma.

I definitely feel more whole, closer to myself, less inhibited. But I have also experienced a certain amount of paranoia smoking hashish. It brings me so much into the present I feel as if I have had a series of blackouts. Some hash is golden and refines everything. I learn that you have to be careful about the quality of what you smoke. As more and more circulates, the dodgier it becomes.

I never smoke a joint with Tony. We get high naturally on each other. Some of my friends change radically after they start taking drugs.

HE STANDS IN PURPLE AND DENIM WITH A CURTAIN OF SILVER FOR A SHAWL. AND TALKS OF LOVE AND LSD...Cardboard sandals tied to his feet and pink chiffon knotted to his neck. There's a gap where his two front teeth used to be. Over the heath he goes laughing and leaping, tall in the lilac dusk. And an aeroplane tears a hole in the sky.

Sitting in the dew on a silver curtain, reflected in the sky in the pond, he tells a legend of how he took a trip and thought he saw a vision of a man riding a white horse. But it wasn't a vision, it was real, and the policeman on the horse said, "What are you doing here?" Amazed by it all, he simply replied, "Man, what a beautiful horse you have. What a beautiful horse." And the policeman smiled and now a knight galloped away into the night that was no longer starless.

He tosses a bottle of lemonade to his lips, throws stones and blows his nose on a leaf. Pretends he's a statue on a wall and a maniac crouching in a bush. Wants to go the fun fair that is locked.

And later, on the platform where silver trains crash in, he shows the colours of his topaz ring in the softness of a match. He has a ring on every finger.

Then he floats away on a silver bird reading a nursery comic and doesn't worry about where he is going.

This is the last time I saw Bob Coffee who two years earlier had been a smartly dressed ladies' hairdresser, living in a posh house in Finchley. I hear he has moved to Cornwall and become a binman.

Fragment Ten: The Brightest Star In The Sky

WHEN I go back home my parents have no choice but to accept Tony as part of my life. They grow fond of him, but they can see no future in the relationship. I hardly ever think about the future or try to plan. It is in my nature to live free like a Gypsy. I can remember when I was just old enough to read, staring at advertisements inside train carriages. There was one for Abbey National life insurance showing a couple carrying an umbrella made of a brick roof. Even then this had irked me.

After work I usually catch the train to Baker Street and then the Metropolitan Line to Finchley Road. Tony is waiting for me by the ticket office. I never wear a watch and my timekeeping is erratic. Almost without fail he is still there waiting for me, even if I get caught up in something and am a couple of hours late. He has nothing else to do but wait for me. I never wonder how he spends his time. I am too busy spending my own.

Occasionally he takes me to the cinema and sits with his long legs stretched out over the row of seats in front. He laughs loudly at anything that is amusing.

His favourite actors are Steve McQueen and Jack Palance. He is also a great fan of Peter O'Toole who has recently filmed *Lawrence of Arabia*. He is fascinated by the directness of O'Toole's gaze. He once passed him in the street in Hampstead and looked into his incredibly blue eyes. He said it made him feel funny.

Maddy worships Oliver Reed. She travels to fleapits all over London to see him in 'B' movies, playing werewolves and villains. She bumps into him outside Finchley Road Station and asks for his autograph. He scribbles it inside the paperback he is carrying, tears out the page and hands it to her with a cheeky grin. Maddy is ecstatic.

Tony crushes me in his arms as if he hasn't seen me for weeks. We melt into each other.
Everything in the station entrance is suddenly happening in slow motion. Our hearts race.

There are so many rooms to choose from. All he needs is a small deposit. They aren't fussy about who they take. I remember endless flights of stairs and junk shop furniture. Beds thousands of people have slept on.

I don't care. I know I can leave any time.

One room he rents is in a house owned by a gay couple. It is incredibly neat and tidy. The linen is as white as snow and there is every utensil anyone could possibly ever need in the cutlery drawer. I catch sight of a sink on the landing, behind a frilly curtain. They peg up pairs of rubber gloves of various colours for different chores.

The nastiest place Tony finds is in long, straight road near Swiss Cottage. The tall, grey house belongs to an old man and his daughter. They get drunk and have rows on the stairs.

However humble the surroundings, in the twilight we can be anywhere. We listen to pop music on a transistor. The Beatles' song *Michelle* is one of Tony's favourites.

I knock on the peeling front door one afternoon and the old man sets upon me. He is drunk as usual. His daughter joins him in the hall as I force my way upstairs. He accuses me of being a slut.

"We know what you do up there!" he shouts ."We've found contraceptives in the wastepaper basket!" yells his daughter. I tell them what I think of the poor condition of the room and their drinking habits. They have been waiting for the opportunity to creep out of the basement like big spiders. Although I put on a brave face the attack deeply upsets me and I refuse to go there again.

On scraps of paper I sometimes scribble down how I feel:

'Unable to believe in you as you stand there. Gasping silently as you move across my path. There is a shimmering on this afternoon; and the sky is very high over the woods burnished with summer.

Perhaps if I had seen the Resurrection is would have been like this? We stand front to front, a few feet apart, with only the grass between us. The grass is growing greener with our moments. And we run forward to meet ourselves for shelter on this eternal afternoon.

You say how tolerant I am because I do not mind the mud. And we race, and you pull me down on some dry grass, and we clamber up for it is full of hidden water. The grass is crying tears. It must know of the future.

Together we swim on the wind as the kites fly with us, blind to nothing: going to look at a big, dead museum of a house. Peering through the windows at the ornamental furniture, we have tea instead and then returning to the dusty room eat corn floating in butter; and flow again into the other, while the afternoon dying lives on though long dead....'

I have an impacted wisdom tooth. My dentist removes it while I am fully awake in the chair. This is more difficult than he anticipates. He breaks the tooth into four sections. I am in the chair all afternoon. Afterwards my bottom lip remains numb because of the depth of the incision. He has damaged the nerves. When Tony kisses me part of his kiss is missing. The dentist assures me that the sensation will gradually return.

I'm not well enough to go to work. Tony comes to the house, sits on the bedroom floor and reads me extracts from *Winnie the Pooh*.

When my parents are away on holiday Clive stays in his old bedroom with Fran. Tony and I sleep in my room. We play *Where Did Our Love Go?* by the Supremes.

Clive and Tony show a distant respect for each other. Clive is jealous of Tony's relationship with me. Tony would have got closer to Clive if he had allowed this to happen. But Clive always acts in a superior way, always gives the impression that he has to take care of urgent business. He always calls Tony *Man*.

Sometimes Clive treats Fran like a slave. She is a fantastic cook and produces delicious spaghetti bolognaise. She says little, just stares at me with her cow eyes.

Years later, when Clive is trying to trace Fran, he writes c/o her brother, asking to see her. He is traumatised when he receives a letter explaining that after being admitted to a mental hospital, some considerable time ago, she had committed suicide. When he told me, I tried to dismiss it, so he wouldn't be too upset. Afterwards, I bitterly regretted my lukewarm response.

Clive adores Fran in the same way as I adore Tony. When she left him to go abroad on a dancing contract he was heartbroken. I remember him crying, the tears falling down his face.

But she seemed to have encouraged him to become more excessive and unstable, just looked on with those unfathomable eyes.

Tony and I go on holiday together. We hitchhike overnight to the Lake District in lorries. Tony makes conversation with the drivers who pick up hikers to relieve their boredom.

They welcome our ghostly silhouettes waiting in the yellow light at roundabouts in the middle of nowhere with a hold-all.

We stay at bed and breakfasts, leading for the first time in our relationship the semblance of a normal married life.

During the day we fly-fish from little rowing boats. I am impressed by how green the grass is and the watercolour lakes.

We take black and white photographs. In some I am wearing a mini skirt made of navy and white striped cotton, and one of Tony's jumpers, grey with a rolled neck. I enjoy the feel of it touching my skin because it has touched him. I have wooden sandals with leather straps across the toes. When it rains I wear tight, pale blue cotton trousers, a navy-blue jacket and a pink silk headscarf.

I get a lovely shot of Tony nuzzling with a horse. We capture our reflection in a small, round mirror while going over the Forth Bridge in a coach. At Lake Windermere I pose in a bikini. He poses in his wet jeans, standing in the water, showing off his Michelangelo torso.

We climb a hill and make love halfway up in a field. Tony is happy, *most of the time*.

I am glad that he is so passionate. It would be awful if he had been indifferent, ignored me, dropped off to sleep, done a crossword puzzle.

We hitchhike up the east coast to Northumbria. He swims in the ice-cold sea and does press-ups on the pebbles. I put my toe in. We visit Holy Island, Lindisfarne, reachable by a causeway when the tide is out. We stay the night in an old hotel. It is a strange, creepy place with a view of a ruined priory. Polanski used the island as the location for his haunting movie *Cul De Sac.* The gulls shriek and the wind stunts everything it touches.

We make love on Holy Island in the afternoon. Sometimes he whispers obscenities but makes them sound as pure as extracts from the Mass.

After Holy Island we go to Scotland via Berwick-Upon-Tweed. It is raining in Berwick, and we escape the puddles in an empty cinema screening a Jack Palance movie. In Edinburgh Tony shows me the theatre where he performed, and we explore the castle. He snaps me sitting on a canon.

When we arrive back home, early in the morning, my father cooks us eggs and bacon and fried bread. He is staggered when Tony devours a whole loaf.

Vic develops and enlarges the photographs in his dark room when I go back to work. I write about Tony at the office, on copy paper.

'The brightest star in the sky, Sirius, fascinated him. At one time he was writing a book called after the star.

Like the bright star, mirrors and windowpanes full of stars taunted him. Deceptive and fragile, he found his release in smashing them. Everywhere he lived he smashed a window, this tall youth as naked as the grey boy who stands above the traffic at Hyde Park.

His eyes were vulnerable as two blue windows that people could so easily smash with their thoughts and actions. People worried him.

He loved the graceful way she-cats moved, how tom cats prowled - outcasts like himself, he must have thought.

The trees, he said, were sometimes beckoning to him. He was always noticing the sky. How it changed colour, standing still in the street to watch, while others hurried by. He came down the steps on winter or summer mornings and became a shepherd with a sailor's walk as he had love affairs with open spaces, shattered mirror puddles with his feet, and breathed in the fresh air so deeply that it made him dizzy.

He was a prince and a beggar of a world of his own making.

Some people said: "He must be the HAPPIEST person in the world!" They heard him singing as he strode along. Others, who had seen his other side, hated him. To them he was a mountain of rage and egotism with his booming voice and actorly gestures. For sometimes every word was four-lettered. Yet sometimes he was gentle as a child and kind. He'd run and fetch and carry for you, just like a child, to please…'

Often Tony went all the way home with me, at least an hour's journey on the train and a bus. We dawdled up the sloping suburban street and he kissed me outside the front gate. Then he went all the way back to Hampstead, alone.

Afterwards I recalled how we stood so close together on the chilly platform at Finchley Road. Our breath steamed and floated up to the ice stars. He enveloped me in his duffle coat.

A few times he has been desperate to make love to me when he is homeless, sleeping on friends' floors, or sitting up all night in the laundrette. I stay with him in a flat that belongs to an artist. He is married with children and there are murals of the family in every room. The painted people stare at us from the walls.

Once he even dragged a mattress down in a derelict basement full of dry leaves and invisible rats.

Flattered by his unquenchable desire and disturbed by it, I sometimes thank God that I can go home to suburbia and escape his extremes.

For a while he shares a pad with some students. One has long red hair down to his waist. He wears purple shirts and his hair is full of lice. Tony has to treat himself for crabs.

We feel that when we make love we are exuding the purest light.

Fragment 11: Porridge

JIM Ramble is the complete opposite of Tony. He appears in my office one morning seeking publicity for his client, the talented Georgie Fame. He is extremely cool and charming. He has short, light brown hair, twinkling blue eyes and a hard jaw and mouth. He has become a publicist via the unusual route of doing a stretch in prison. He shows me the split in the lining of his leather jacket where someone tried to stab the previous owner. The jacket was a gift.

He is public schoolboy, son of a tea planter. He went to prison after staging a daring and sophisticated robbery at an art gallery. After he knows me for a while he shows me the press cuttings from the front pages of the nationals. His stretch in prison accounts for his hard expression.

He always carries wads of money and travels everywhere in cabs charged to the business. I like him a lot but not enough to be unfaithful to Tony. Jim is divorced and lives a bachelor life in small, expensive apartments with intercoms and porters.

It is exciting being picked up by him at the office after work. There is no limit on what we can do. He wraps his sheepskin coat around my shoulders on cold evenings. I feel protected. When he is going to be late meeting me under the clock at Victoria Station, I am greeted by a personal announcement over the tannoy system.

I can't help feeling uplifted when I am within his powerful magnetic field.

I write a piece about Georgie Fame: *'A healthy, mountain-tanned Georgie Fame is back from a skiing holiday in the Tyrol. He had a great time trying out the slopes and getting some fresh air into his lungs.*

"We were growing rather worried about the boy," his publicist told me. "He kept lying down groaning and had bags under his eyes. So we pushed him off."

His manager is Rik Gunnell, owner of the Flamingo Club in Wardour Street, which Georgie has made such a popular hangout. Rik bought him a Mark 2 Jaguar as a present for making the sensational entry in the Top Ten with Yeh! Yeh!

Georgie Fame, 24, real name Clive Powell, left school at fifteen with the choice of either working in the cotton mills of Lancashire or choking away down a coal mine. He chose the mills but only a year later was a full-time musician. His father, a pub pianist, encouraged Georgie to start piano lessons at the age of seven.'

Later Jim arranges for me to interview Georgie at his pad, a mews house in Chelsea:

'Finding Fame was not as easy as I thought. We arrived outside. The problem? There was no bell or knocker. After a search, communication with the inside still eluded us, and we decided upon a light blow on the small door, with a fist.

The door flew open immediately. A beautiful girl in Levi's and a maroon skinny sweater, asked us in, as she flicked back her long, thick hair.

"Everyone always asks where the bell is," she said. "There isn't one actually. Most of our friends knock on the window."

The living room was untidy and looked as if they had been having 'a bit of a rave up'.

Carmen, the long-haired chick is Georgie's girl. With another slim, cropped-headed girl in bleached Levi's, she is busy tidying the pad.

"Clive shouldn't be long," said Carmen, banging a cushion into shape.

"The place is a mess because we've been away for a while. Friends tend to move in and take over."

Soon a huge American car appeared outside the window, and Georgie noisily parked in the narrow street.

He entered straight-faced in a suede coat and cute sheepskin hat with flaps, and then disappeared up the small flights of stairs. Both girls pulled faces as if to say, "Get him!"

He wasn't being rude though, just a little preoccupied, and soon curled up beside me on the sofa and said, "I thought I was going to miss this interview. I'm glad I didn't."

We talked about the two new albums he was working on before his holiday in Austria.

"Listen to this," he said, leaping up, going to record player on the floor. "It's different from anything we've recorded before. We're working with Denny Cordell (he records the Moody Blues) and he's got some great ideas."

The number was Sitting In The Park, a super track.

Not long after that Denny Cordell turned up in person with hair ruffled, wearing Levi's, and with a stack of records under his arm.

"Is it true you're still not interested in making commercial records?" I asked Georgie.

"No, not anymore. Not after I had a Number One with Yeh! Yeh! I don't think the singles I have brought out since then have had exciting enough treatment. Anyway, look how many good commercial numbers there are in the charts now."

What about food? I remember seeing a picture of you in a paper putting something into an oven. Do you cook?"

"Well they dragged me out of bed to take that when my record hit the top. I was half asleep at the time.

"I was brought up on stodge. You know, potato pie and stuff like that. I like it but it's bad for you. There is a great restaurant near here where they do kebabs."

"Clothes?"

"I do wear a lot of suede gear but I gave up buying suede jackets after I had a couple nicked. I like well-cut suits, and buy casual stuff in Carnaby Street. For my winter sports holiday I wore ordinary ski pants.

"The air in Austria is a gas. You can go to bed terribly late, get up a seven, and just one breath of mountain air puts you right back on your feet again. The night life is fast-moving too."

Georgie's house is rented. It's quaint. There are lots of dolls around, and a grandfather clock that permanently says five past six. There's a piano and two cool pictures of Georgie at either end. One of Georgie's favourite toys is a shoulder-high doll with long, gangling limbs, a pointed nose like a carrot and a fur moustache.

"I found it here with a load of stuff in the basement. My heart went over when I saw it. I thought it was a dead body!" grinned Georgie.

The Fame band are one of the hardest working units on the music scene. They often do seven nights a week.

Time is making demands again and Georgie and Denny disappear into the London traffic in the conspicuous American car. Denny slips a single into the record player...'

Another of Jim's clients is an extremely confident, former university student who has penned a song called *It's Good News Week* for a bunch of RAF recruits called Hedgehoppers Anonymous. They enjoy five-minute stardom. Then Jonathan King writes and records his enchanting hit *Everyone's Gone To The Moon.*

He arrives at my office for an interview, skinny and enthusiastic, with big glasses and white, tight-fitting cord trousers. He is a real show-off but likeable.

Clive

Fragment 12: A Place To Drop In

PEOPLE continually drop into my office. Some will become famous. Some will have a small taste of fame. Some will die. Others have nothing better to do.

There is no security, only Shirley on the switchboard, and she gives everyone a wonderful, open smile, has the largest, bluest of eyes. Later she changes and becomes much more cynical and guarded. She discovers that the girls she has booked in for interviews are applying for *her job*. The vacancy for a telephonist has been advertised without even letting Shirley know of her pending dismissal. When she discovers what has happened she loses her temper and goes upstairs and thumps with all her might on Reg Taylor's desk. Soon she becomes manageress of an employment agency and reveals a whole different side to her personality.

At this point in time she is my protectress. She vets my phone calls and brings in cups of coffee for pop stars. This gives her a chance to peek at them and seductively flap her long eyelashes, heavy with mascara.

I snare an extremely handsome American actor into the office. Ben Carruthers is appearing in the new movie, *The Dirty Dozen,* with a whole host of stars. When I receive the publicity pictures from the film company and see how good looking he is, I decide to interview him out of sheer curiosity. Shirley trips in, after a few seconds of his arrival, pretending to be my personal assistant.

"Coffee or tea?" she asks the exceedingly dishy actor, demurely.

"Coffee, with cream," smiles the laid-back American, and that of course has destroyed the illusion we want to create. All that is available in the staff kitchen is a bottle of pasteurised milk!

Ben Carruthers is gorgeous, with curly brown hair and magnificent dark eyes. After the interview I walk with him down Oxford Street to the tube. He doesn't seem to be aware of how amazing he is and is surprisingly natural. He tells me he is about to make a movie with iconic actress Susannah York, and then disappears down an escalator, placing his shades in position.

This is the point in my life when I can have almost anyone I want. But I never consider being unfaithful to Tony. I love him so intensely, not even this American movie star, if he *were* looking for a girlfriend, could upstage him.

I have my birth chart drawn up by an astrologer.

'Neptune in Libra conjunct with the Fifth House, the nature of your deepest spiritual yearnings and most elevated ideals.

The ideals of your generation centre on marriage due to the passage of Neptune in Libra between 1942 and 1957. Many of you sought, or still seek, an impossible level of perfection in love, a divine union. Hence many of you are reluctant to tie yourself down to one imperfect partner forever, whilst others married young, under illusion, and boosted the high divorce statistics of the generation. But don't forget you are part of "the beautiful people" who worship harmony, love and peace, through songs, art, fashion, film, and meditation. Your vision is one of social justice and racial and sexual equality.

On a more personal level, you are in some way a romantic fool or an idealist, prey to delusion and yet willing to give up your ego and merge with your lover. In the same way you can be like an actor who really lives a part, rather than just plays it ...'

Michael Caine drops in with some photographs. He is eager for the publicity. He is Clive's friend and I have met him socially on a number of occasions. Michael and Clive worked together in a TV play, *Goodbye Charlie*, and also shared being out of work. They killed time by going to see movies in the afternoons, eating bags of apples in the back row.

Michael is thirty and seems quite mature. Many of the highly successful people I interview are still in their teens or early twenties. He has already appeared as the arrogant British officer in *Zulu a*nd is tipped to become as big as James Bond when he appears as Harry Palmer in *The Ipcress File*, due to be released shortly.

I have visited his home and met his mum and brother. I have eaten with him and Clive at "in" restaurants and at the Pickwick Club - laughed at his jokes. But I am still rather in awe of him and thrilled that he brings the photos to my office to go with the piece I am writing.

'Aside from taking a calculating stroll on the acting scene Mr Caine is aware of the importance of studying his private life. For instance he spent many hours selecting the décor for his mews house near Marble Arch. And the other day I came across him buying a super tape recorder in a shop in Shaftesbury Avenue.

"I really dig the pop scene," he said with a direct look from those blue eyes (he's obviously thought about that too, about the way he drops his eyelids, and looks slowly up again).

"I think of myself as being one step ahead of the hit parade. I buy a record I think is great. Nine times out of ten it makes it."

Michael has a great sense of humour and a great laugh. The sort of laugh that makes you want to laugh some more. You get the feeling in his company that you are being well looked after.

I asked him the sort of treatment a girl is likely to expect from him on a date. He took a long puff of a French cigarette, paused..

"Firstly I'm jealous. If I go dancing I don't expect my girl to dance with other fellas. If she so much as glances at another guy I'm off home. And I never bother to see her again. But with me a girl never has any responsibilities. I hate the idea of going Dutch. I wouldn't take a girl out, if I couldn't afford it." '

When I was eighteen Clive had become close friends with both Michael and Terry Stamp. I went to the house they shared in Ebury Street, Victoria. Michael sat under an ornate canopy, and while waiting to become famous, was writing a play on a portable typewriter.

Another of their friends is singer Doug Sheldon who recorded *Run Around Sue*. Rumour has it that when he drives around Sloane Square in his sports car with the hit song blaring out, he jerks his coolly booted leg up over the door as the number reaches a crescendo.

One afternoon, in Kensington, Clive introduced me to model April Ashley who was once a young sailor. She'd had sexual reassignment surgery. She was extremely beautiful with a husky voice. Her brown eyes smouldered beneath sweeping false lashes.

I am in awe of Terry when I first meet him.

'The piercing blue eyes, which fix penetratingly on you can be most unnerving,' I write. *'His walk is male and powerful. His longish hair blows up slightly as he goes around London with a new script running through his head.*

He has a lean look and a panther tread. He can be tough and hard and yet remarkably kind and considerate to those he likes and respects.

Even though his work is the most important thing in his life, he takes an enormous interest in girls. Watching them walking up and down Regent Street from a taxi window, he said, "If you spent a lifetime, you'd never get to know all of them."

He took as naturally to swish living as he did to the celluloid - when he performs a scene in a film he likes to get it over in just one take, and usually does this most successfully.

Everything he wears is of the best and one of his favourite activities is connected with food, he spends many hours walking around delicatessens with a large wicker basket. And one of his biggest kicks is to order a huge hamper of tuck from Harrods and share it with his friends.

Most of his free time is spent with his girl, beautiful model Jean Shrimpton. He says that if he were the marrying kind he'd marry her tomorrow.

At present he's working on the new film Modesty Blaise. *His evenings are spent relaxing in his flat in Mayfair, where he has an impressive collection of books, modern jazz and antiques.*

Clive often drops in at the office. We always have a lot to talk about, in depth. It is strange how eventually he became so silent. He wanders in when I am interviewing a group called the Rats. One of them has a huge chunk of cheese and sits nibbling while I ask questions.

David Bowie, looking hardly more than a schoolboy, drops in with his manager. Three years later he will record *Space Oddity*. We squeeze in a few lines about him in the weekly gossip column *Heads and Tales.*

'David, leader of the Lower Third, has designed himself a grey suit with an imperial military cut and a row of crowned brass buttons down the front and a high black suede collar. This is going to be featured by John Stephen's boutique along with a shirt with a pleated front.

John has suggested that ex-art student David should design some similar lines for girls. But he's totally against it.

"I like my women very feminine," he said.'

The legendary Marc Bolan also makes a brief appearance on the other side of my desk, with cropped hair, looking even younger than David.

Donovan drops in with his girlfriend Sarah, a golden-haired beauty at art school. He levers off a large suede boot and makes himself comfortable.

"Don't mind me taking it off?" he asks. The small, curly headed folk singer offers me a Polo mint.

On top of the hair is perched a small, dark blue sailcloth cap. He wears a red and black polo neck sweater, a navy donkey jacket and jeans.

The Press have accused him of copying Bob Dylan. He has appeared on *Ready Steady Go!* singing his song *Catch The Wind.* A sign on his acoustic guitar reads, *This Machine Kills*.

"I just want to keep going," he explains, gazing with innocent blue eyes into a future of hitchhiking and moving along the road.

"Show business for me is just a stopping point on the journey. I want the money so that I'll have enough to write the stuff I want to write. Money doesn't mean much. I don't use a lot of things, but I've bought a new guitar and some LPs."

Donovan's younger brother is still at school.

"But he'll turn out to be an ordinary guy with a steady job," Donovan assures me.

"My Dad understood when I went roaming that it was something I had to do. He's well-read but works in a factory. Odd isn't it? I think everyone should be able to hear folk music. One of my ambitions is to bring out a new label catering exclusively for Folk.

At the moment I'm looking for a pad somewhere in Chelsea. Two small rooms, bathroom and kitchen. Don't know of any, do you?"

I shake my head.

A couple of months later I drop in at Donovan's new dive. I have to ring the bell twice, the code that I am friendly.

Gypsy Dave, Donovan's roady, opens the door of this Kensington pad. Donovan greets me wearing a felt cloak with a metal clasp at the neck.

'In the spacious lounge groovy people are draped around on the furniture. In the corner Bob Dylan stares sideways from a huge, black and white photograph rolled and curled so that it stands up. People coming in remark about it, change the shape a bit.

A girl with long hair, wearing a black hipster skirt with a straw belt, gets up and does a jerky little dance with Don who passes the cloak to a friend. His jeans are so worn they look as if they've seen a thousand days of living rough.

A few moments before Don had been sitting ecstatically on the edge of a sofa, grinning and digging some great vocals that have been recorded on a tiny machine. A tall girl arrives in toeless boots and white trousers and a corduroy reefer jacket and begins to paint, picking out the colours from little bottles on the coffee table.

Someone puts on a Bob Dylan LP, and a youth wanders in and out, pale-faced and golden-haired, wearing beautifully tapered jeans.

A girl sits in a corner and doesn't say a word for two hours.

I wander around the flat and peep into a number of untidy bedrooms. A beautiful baby is sleeping in a cot.

After Gypsy Dave has persuaded everyone to smell a bag of jasmine tea, he makes coffee in a Chinese teapot and I help wash some cups in the bathroom, because the kitchen sink is full of soaking nappies. There are at least thirty empty milk bottles lined up.

"How many people live here?" I ask Gypsy Dave.

"Officially five," he grins. "There's Diane and her husband Paul, who's Don's friend, and their baby, and me and Don. Diane gets a bit mad because we say we'll eat out and then come in and start wolfing up all their food."

They eat pineapple out of a tin with forks. The juice is passed round in a wine glass. The girl in the white slacks has taken off her boots and is painting her feet different colours. Dick from the Pretty Things drifts in from nowhere, alters Dylan's picture and leaves.

A small boy with long hair comes in and offers round a half-eaten Wimpy.

"Where's Don?" someone asks suddenly. "He's very tired and has jacked it in and gone to bed."

I hang out in Donovan's dressing room before he appears on *Ready Steady Go.* Gypsy Dave has just washed his hair and goes out into the television studio with it still wet. The air reeks of marijuana. Gypsy offers me a drag. I follow them into the blinding glare of the studio lamps, merging with the colour and excitement and stifled fear of broadcasting live.

Mick Jagger is sitting at the edge of the platform contemplating the scene. He is wearing a greeny-blue roll neck jumper and brown slacks.

I visit various studios where pop shows are televised. Glittering phantoms still haunt me. Sandie Shaw singing *There's Always Something There To Remind Me* with bare feet. The Righteous Brothers performing *You've Lost That Loving Feeling* in a golden spotlight. Tina Turner's hard, brown legs as she belts out *River Deep And Mountain High* with Ike, on Top Of The Pops.

I meet *Radio Caroline* DJ, Simon Dee at a reception and he invites me out for lunch. I'm not keen on going. He's not really my type, rather smooth with a corny sense of humour. He has promised to play me a request on his show.

He takes me to a steak bar and we drink so much wine that the room begins to spin like a turntable. Soon Simon's affable personality gets him into TV where his chat show scores high ratings. He begins dating the most glamorous women in London.

I hid in the loo when he came to take me to lunch but Shirley had blown my cover. He never played my request.

I attend an unforgettable reception at EMI for the entire Tamla Motown stable who give interviews during their first visit to England. They are so happy and bubbly and have brought their families along.

Little Stevie Wonder who is 15, is with his tutor. He seems to be the happiest of all and not at all concerned about being blind. His face lights up behind his dark glasses. He tells me he has been *sightseeing.*

Fragment 13: Searching For Matches In Empty Boxes

CLIVE'S friend Lee Harris is a South African Jew. He is charming and empathetic. A teacher and a social worker he has his finger on the pulse of all that is happening at the highest and lowest levels of London life. *Darting around, buzzing with thoughts, tumbling with sentences, searching for matches in empty boxes. Waking from dreams which end with someone crying.*

Clive is private and mysterious, closely guards his secrets. People are intrigued and drawn to him like a magnet. This is a dangerous quality but eventually Clive is his own, most profoundly damaged victim.

'The wind blows back his dark, curly hair from his forehead and a scarf wound round his neck could never strangle his adventures. Behold him, the young adventurer, delving into mysteries that he finds in places that others ignore as ordinary.

One evening he was chatting to a toothless old hag who feeds the birds in squares. He found her, this piece of human rubbish, discarded by the world, going through the garbage, sifting out the waste food from the papers and pieces of glass. She stood with her baskets at her feet, filled by dustbin not supermarket, and told him marvellous stories about pigeons.

"There's Peg Leg," she said. "He walks on two stumps. He lost his feet in the tar. They all have names." She flew lightly from beak to feather to personality. He flew with her.

You will find him adventuring in all kinds of odd places, with all kinds of people. Dipping his fingers into cesspools and bringing out gold.'

Clive and Lee take me to various gay clubs in Soho.

I sip wine, watch massive men who look like truck drivers smouch with slender, made-up boys who are more feminine than women. I am conscious of how much they need each other as they cling together on tiny, crowded dance floors drowned by excessively loud pop music. I see *Passion*, exposed and vulnerable, wearing men's garments but nothing at all to do with gender. Are they seeking mothers, or fathers, or parts of their hearts that they have broken or lost?

Mr Barker has written several books. One of them is *Nerves And Their Cure*, which my mother has read avidly and underlined certain passages.

'Sexual inhibitions, fears and phobias, reveal another form of nervous trouble and are responsible for a great deal of suffering. Some women are frigid, some men are impotent, not because nature has made them so, or disease has ravaged them but because one part of their personality is saying "yes" to sex expression just as another part of the personality is saying "no".'

In another book, Psychology's Impact On The Christian Faith, published in 1964, he writes: *'We are just emerging from an era when any mention of sex was considered completely out of place. Many people suppose that now we are reaching the opposite extreme. When, as was the case in ancient Greece and Rome, sex reached a kind of saturation point where it produced cynicism. If you have a swing of the pendulum on one side you will naturally have it on the other with equally unfortunate results. If one generation refuses to acknowledge the goodness of sex it is not likely that we shall get a balanced view in the next.*

We will remember the stir caused in 1962 by the court case concerned with the publication of Lady Chatterley's Lover. The worst that such a publication could do was to give adolescents, and others who were interested, an unvarnished account of sexual intercourse.'

Clive, Lee and I go to clubs in London where we dance with rows of girl-boys and boy-girls to *My Guy* by Mary Wells and where a blaze of elation and warmth pervades every space between the jubilant dancers. They are wonderful company, free spirits.

And those who don't belong, belong because they don't belong and nobody belongs and yet belongs as the shining music throbs us into being more than we believe.

When we are walking around Soho late at night, Clive and Lee are protective towards me. But in most parts of the city there is little fear of violence and we move around freely. Clive and I often walk home from central London to the suburbs if we miss the last train. We walk into the dawn, drawing energy from our youth and belief in the impossible.

Clive takes me to a strip joint. He warns me that people will assume I am a lesbian. There is a woman with huge breasts that look as if they have been pumped up. A girl with ebony limbs snaps her fingers and gives off electric shocks as she gyrates on an excuse for a stage. I view the strippers with detachment. They seem sad and defeated, more clinical than erotic. I feel sorry for them. They have the lacklustre of wild animals stuck in a circus. Afterwards I wondered why Clive took me there.

The gays I know on the pop scene hang out with John Stephen. They include Long John Baldry, a highly respected club singer. The six foot seven inch giant releases a poignant single *Let The Heartaches Begin*.

Lee is offered an Arts Council grant and writes *Love Play*. It is about a young Mod who gets high on LSD. He wants it to be performed in a cathedral but accepts the Arts Laboratory, a trendy venue for experimental art.

Fragment 14: Help!

THE Beatles' movie Help! is being shot at Twickenham Studios. I go there with a bunch of photographers. Fans have scrawled the boys' names all over the studio gates.

I find myself standing in a street that looks like Coronation Street. On one side houses are painted on canvas. On the other there are actual houses but the upstairs and roofs are missing.

From inside comes scuffling and laughing and snatches of the Beatles saying their lines. Then a strange little man who looks like an Arab, with a rag tied round his head and wearing a long skirt with a suit jacket, pads down the street in sandals.

"Who brought *that* in?" one of the photographers jokes. But the funny little man ignores him.

Next to arrive are four cups of tea. And Brian Epstein bursts through the front of one of the canvas houses with some LPs under his arm and disappears again.

I am dying to get a glimpse of the Beatles. When I do it seems unreal.

'They looked gorgeous!' I write. 'Very tanned – partly make-up – and were clowning around. They were all there except Ringo. When Ringo did appear he walked up to George and John and shook hands and said, "How are you?" as if he hadn't seen them for years. Everyone roared with laughter.

Paul was a wearing a tweed jacket and polo neck sweater. George had on a pink shirt and his hair was thick and shiny. John looked broad and masculine in his reefer jacket. And

Ringo couldn't resist playing with the photographers' cameras while they were trying to take pictures of him.'

The first time I see the Beatles live is at the Hammersmith Odeon when they are on tour with Cilla Black. Don Higgs, an intrepid reporter I work with on the weekly newspaper, wangles us in free, flashing our NUJ press cards. The screams still ring in my ears.

The national love affair with the group turns global and never stops. *HELP!* is much more than a pop song. I feel it has been specially written for complex people like Tony and Clive.

Won't you help me get my feet back on the ground? Won't you PLEASE help me?

My friend George, who lives fifteen minutes away by mini van, has a theory that the Beatles have been beamed in from some higher dimension to wake up humanity. There is no point in sending saints and martyrs when people are no longer religious. But they can relate to groups playing pop songs.

But this isn't entirely true. My father's heart turns to stone. He says he now knows what the atomic bomb is for. He still lives in the Twenties, wearing wide trousers with unfashionable turn-ups!

My mother reacts differently. For her the Sixties offer an opportunity to find out who she is. She appears at the kitchen table at 2am, unable to sleep, and shares joints with our friends who take refuge there after parties. Sometimes my father fights his way through the fog and orders them out.

A revolution is going on, quietly and discreetly in suburbia. George and I, under the influence of marijuana, creep into the park and steal some deck chairs. We think it's terribly funny.

George is tall and angular, wears horn-rimmed glasses. He has beautiful, kind, brown eyes. He turns up at the house to hang out with my "groovy" mother. Everything that is meaningful in George's world is either "groovy" or "knock-out!"

He is good at languages and gets a job with a travel company as a tour guide. He takes LSD in a field in Austria and comes home with an amazing account of how he has communicated with a cow. He starts wearing beads and grows his hair long. He decides to trek round India and writes me long, interesting letters.

My mother seems to understand what I am going through with Tony. She doesn't condemn his erratic, outrageous behaviour. She understands his vulnerability.

I feel sorry for my mother. My father is a workaholic. When he is not out working he is at home in his office. I am concerned about my mother's need to be encouraged to use her mind and express herself. She feels that being married and bringing up children has never allowed her to do this.

The Beatles speak to different generations. They speak to and on behalf of the Eleanor Rigbys of this world, women like my mother who have not fulfilled their potential.

My mother stifles how she feels. Her GP makes it easier by handing out purple hearts, Valium, and sleeping pills. As far back as I can remember my mother has experienced difficulty sleeping. She is petrified of going to sleep, letting go. Valium is considered to be a wonder drug. It makes visits to psychoanalysts like Mr Barker unnecessary. Valium muffles everything like invisible snow. Obsessive thoughts lie buried and frozen.

My grandmother gave birth to fifteen children. She had hardly any time to nurse one before another was on her lap. They grew up and had families of their own. My mother was probably one of the most sensitive. An eccentric uncle lives at the top of my grandmother's house. He comes down to chat whenever we make an impromptu visit. Bert is different from my other uncles and has worked out his own strange, personal philosophy.

I am fascinated by Bert.

'Look for wisdom and perhaps you will find it here? Here is where he has built his hermit's cave in a gloomy, Victorian house. In his room at the top, he has completely revolutionised the day. He cooks eggs and bacon at 2am and sleeps in the light. And when he feels inclined throws his washing water from a bowl out of the window.

Intriguing you will find him because although he pretends stupidity he'll pick your wits with needles to confirm ideas he already has. And oh! what marvellous fantasies he has had time to event.

Ill-health, a gammy leg has kept him there for years. Alone he has passed his youth away. He slices the canvas uppers of his bumper boots to allow his toes to breathe, and safety-pins his trousers.

He sends strange cuttings through the post and reads the Evening Standard from cover to cover, and wonders.

They say he's lazy, that his leg is an excuse for not working, but he's been through butchery in hospital wards. If it is purely laziness it must be a struggle to be lazy. He chews each mouthful twenty times before he swallows. Sends the best Christmas cards out of the entire family, whom he rarely sees, and who never see him.'

When my grandmother dies Bert goes to pieces. He manages to find me before the funeral, in my grandmother's crowded parlour. He is breathless and panic-stricken and sits like a shadow in the shiny black car.

They sell the house. Bert has nowhere to go. He dies the following winter in a hostel.

My mother had always been compassionate, invited him over to the house for lunch. Clive once got him tipsy on ginger wine and whisky, at the pub, for the hell of it.

My grandfather was the total opposite of Bert and had little for time for what he considered his son's weakness. My mother loved her father but admitted they had also been afraid of him. When her brothers had a coal fight in the scullery he rose out of bed in his nightshirt and knocked them all out stone cold.

He was the sort of man that everyone loved because he was so big-hearted. Both grandparents had a terrific sense of humour. All the children inherited it, along with some hidden scars.

My grandmother didn't have a single grey hair, even when she was eighty. Clive used to pick her up as easily as a doll and hold her above his head. She loved it.

My paternal grandmother was a strong woman. Her husband had died when she was young and left her to bring up four sons. Once a mouse dropped down her blouse and she simply pulled it out, without even flinching.

She taught me how to knit. When I was six she knitted me a dressing gown that reached down to my toes, every colour imaginable. But boys were her favourites, especially Clive. She used to bake him jam tarts.

Fragment 15:   A Girl Like A Helter Skelter

HELEN GRIFFITHS is one of my special friends. We meet at college before I become a journalist. On her way to Hornsey Art School she had dropped out for a year to do a secretarial course, for some inexplicable reason. She is totally unsuited to being a secretary but adds a great deal of spice to discussion groups and is incredibly funny.

She is never even slightly bitchy. She is fully open, like a rose, and this open-heartedness makes her whole. Helen isn't pretty but extremely sexy. Her sexuality flows from a direct source, it bubbles up like a fountain. She is in touch with her body, free and not in the least self-conscious or egotistical.

She is short-sighted and without a little pair of spectacles perched on her nose she moves in a blurred landscape that makes her even more spontaneous.

Her frame is small. She has thin legs, strong calf muscles, narrow hips, and a large bust. A mane of thick, chestnut hair flows down her back. Sometimes she scrapes this into a bun which makes her look deceptively efficient, especially with the glasses. She wears tight skirts and tiny stiletto heeled shoes, and clatters around like her own version of Brigitte Bardot. But she has a fine intelligent mouth, not the sensual Bardot pout. She has a sharp mind and is a clown. She loves laughing at herself.

Helen is always in a hurry, one step ahead of where she's going. She carries over her shoulder an enormous leather bag with a long strap, but always mislays books, her shorthand notes, her sense of time.

I find my friendship with Helen healing and liberating. She takes me to chaotic rooms in Hornsey where her art student friends live. I am impressed by their talent and their squalid surroundings. My lack of experience at this point makes me shy in their presence. But I feel I have been taken into an inner sanctum.

Helen has numerous boyfriends. She is amoral. She treats the opposite sex as equal, values herself, is valued. One of her current boyfriends is a good-looking blond. He is the son of Kim Philby, the spy who will soon cause such a sensation because of his activities as a double agent.

Some weekends I stay at Helen's home, where it becomes obvious that she is the way she is because of her laid-back parents.

'*Round and round she goes taking you with her in a spin, a hectic living girl with humour who can live with dust under the bed and under her nose without noticing. She won't wear stockings often and doesn't care about ladders when she does, for boys still run their fingers up her legs for she's got something else that's not synthetic. Her father, a kindly Welshman, fitted loudspeakers all over the rambling house and has a whole room of dusty tapes. He pulled down the kitchen wall and never put it back again because he forgot.*

He never finished anything but never noticed the cracks in the lavatory pan or cobwebs on his thousand books. Never noticed he never noticed. To him his home is a castle although the windows are dirty and the garden overgrown. It is a Land of Song full of lodgers.

He went to Scotland to look after delinquents and left Helen and her younger brother to collect the rents and misbehave. She has a double bed in the front room, always shared and untidy.'

The last time I saw her she was three years more serious and mature. She was madly in love with a charismatic, highly intelligent Black guy and showed him a surprising reverence. They came to my flat in Clapham Common and he rolled joints. Shortly after they left, a policeman called round to get details of a burglary at the flat. It was a narrow escape!

Another of my college friends, Vanessa, has long, curly hair and round, green eyes. She is also ahead of her time and dates Black guys, usually West Indians. It is still rare to see white girls with Black boyfriends. One of the attractions of these guys is the abundant supply of marijuana and hashish they carry around with them. Black people, especially musicians are considered ultra cool.

Vanessa lives at home with her mother – a widow who is a schoolteacher – in a huge flat in Hampstead. She has been raised liberally with a progressive education, and is allowed to use her bedroom, a large, comfortable space with a number of beds, exactly as she pleases. Generally a small crowd gathers there smoking joints and listening to sounds.

Lee, Clive's friend, dates Vanessa. He fits in well in this easy-going atmosphere and charms her mother. I am invited to Vanessa's twenty-first birthday party which is held at the flat. Guests are divided into two quite definite camps – relatives and her mother's friends in the lounge hung with paintings, and Vanessa's friends in the bedroom.

I realise how stoned we are when we troop into the lounge for the cake cutting ceremony. Black guys who have been carving up chunks of hashish temporarily come down to earth while Vanessa attacks her cake with a huge carving knife. Relatives chant happy birthday, oblivious to what is going on.

I am enchanted by Sammy, one of Vanessa's boyfriends. When he dances I am spellbound.

'Sammy has a lithe body. Sammy can dance. He dances as if he were weaving a silver fishing net. As he moves limb and moves limb, he seems to be tacking stitches all around the walls, embroidering the ceiling, bathing us in light as he moves.

Sammy has boots of joy tacked to his black feet. He knows the air around him. He can catch it in his fingers. Sammy just smiles. Sammy just dances.

Rubber limbs chasing shadows that he makes on the floor. A step ahead he dances, conjuring and turning others into cardboard cut-outs. Tops can't spin anymore when he pirouettes. Yellow waistcoat and shining boots of joy, shining skin, shining teeth.

Dance while we stand still Sammy, gasping. Dance far away from your tropical birds and sun. Dance your ballet that has jewels in it. Throw us coconuts full of warm milk as you skip like a flame. Lend us some light. Sammy.'

Vanessa's mother allowed a junkie and his wife to stay at the flat for a few days. He stole milk and yoghurt from the doorstep, after it had been delivered. But he couldn't remember. She empathised, helped him fix, bleed and cry.

Sometimes Vanessa ran into Tony while he was wandering around the Hampstead streets. Neither knew what to say.

Fragment 16: Why My Son?

AT the back of my mind there is always the idea that somehow I can fix Tony, as if he is a broken ornament. I don't think the fixing can be done by giving him more love or understanding or by moving in with him and making him feel safe. My own safety is a priority. I only feel relatively secure if I know I have somewhere to escape, if his mood changes suddenly. He deals with these fluctuations by ordering me to get out in the middle of the night, or leaving me there alone to suffer.

But whenever he becomes indifferent I grow more anxious to see him, creating all sorts of wild fantasies if he fails to call me. My anxiety doesn't subside until I am in his magical arms. Sometimes he disappears.

He gets friendly with a young guy. When I arrive one evening they are examining maps and making plans to go travelling. I feel possessive. The plans fizzle out.

I agonise when he is confused and has a strained expression on his face, also dilated pupils. He is hardly able to contain himself. His emotions begin erupting like lava from a volcano.

'He had his seasons for weeping and laughing and often his tears fell upon her like hot lead. Trees grew unbearably high in the sky which was a bad omen. And the thing that he loved most, freedom, hurt him most. He would come to terms with it for short spells. Tossing through the streets late at night, a storm. Coming back with the wind in his hand. Sitting in the laundrette until dawn broke. Sometimes he was biblical, Cain, his hair ruffled, perspiration glittering above his mouth.

"I'll stay with you if you try and get better," she promised. She tried not to wound him but thought if she impressed on him that he was ill, something miraculous would happen.'

In desperation I go to see Tony's mother. As long as I have known him he has never visited her. She had sent him some money in an envelope with a sad little note. I track her down to where she works in a shop. I imagine that out of all the people in the world she must have some kind of answer.

"Is he in trouble?" is the first thing she says. "He hits you? You musn't put up with that!"

She is nothing like I expect. She is soft and smells of face powder and is confusingly ordinary. And yet though she seems so ordinary when I first hug her, I discover she is leading an unhappy existence. Tony's father died of TB when he was young. He was only seven when he attempted to massage his father's cold limbs back to life. In the early days there had been money and a restaurant. But they were forced to live in a caravan after his death. The air was thick with paraffin fumes. Tony wanted to escape and had left at sixteen.

His mother is living in rented accommodation with her second husband, a little man who is stooped and sleazy. They take me to the pub in the high street and dose me with draught sherry. Afterwards I stand in the kitchen where there is a piano, and she fries sausages. The smell clings to my clothes.

"We thought you'd come because you were pregnant." Her husband uncorks some wine. "I know what's wrong with him," he hints tantalisingly.

We both ask him to reveal his secret. He doesn't.

"I don't know why Tony turned out like this. He was the most popular boy in his class at school." She produces cuttings from the local paper, saying his performance in an end of term play is, 'reminiscent of the great American actor Burt Lancaster'.

"Why my son?"

She shows me school reports and photos of sepia Spanish uncles who had been famous actors in their time.

"He did some terrible things to me before he left home. We won't go into that though. Why my son? He used to have a bad temper when he was small, flew into tantrums. Perhaps it was the bombs that made him cry?"

Tony had shown me a scar on his arm like an arrow wound. He told me his older brother had stuck a knife into him for no reason.

I plead for help. They give me more wine and invite me to stay the night. The room begins to wobble.

"The landlady will fix a room for you. Please stay. We'll talk about it."

Tony's stepfather clutches my arm. He wants to photograph me.

"Don't let him worry you," she retorts. "He wants to take photos of my daughter too. She won't agree. She's very much like you. I went round there last week with a stack of groceries. They wouldn't open the door. Sit down dear. Have another drink. Don't let him worry you."

He uncorks another bottle. The evening is beginning to sway and the curtains are drawn. I am scared.

"I know. I had a long talk with him once," he teases.

Tony used to sit silently on the floor in a corner.

Their invitation changes. Suddenly it's too late to bother the landlady. He suggests I share the double bed with his wife and he will sleep on the imitation leather sofa. But I don't want to sleep with this woman who carried Tony inside her, obscenely jolly, with a sob in her voice.

"Get your coat," she orders, suddenly alarmed, echoing the same words that Tony will use when he bursts into my office.

"We won't take any notice of HIM!"

He runs forward, gripping my arm, begging me to stay.

Tony's mother links arms with me and propels me to the station, desperate to get me away.

"He's so cruel. I'm his third wife. My first husband was a real gentleman, so handsome."

She grows younger as she recalls Tony's father. Everything went threadbare after he died.

"Leave him. Why don't you leave him?" I urge. But I realise she has long given up all thought of movement. Wherever she goes it would make no difference now.

I hug her and kiss her. And the train rushes in to rescue me from another nightmare. I realise, after all, she is only Tony's mother.

Fragment 17: A Photograph of Life

I spend a lot of time with photographers. I envy the way they work, capturing moments as they occur. They can leave with the finished product in their camera bags, unless the film has fogged or the flash failed.

The paparazzi mentality has not yet developed into a serious epidemic. The public still want to see their idols in a kind, as well as glamorous light. At least that is the impression I get on the pop scene. The photographers I meet at receptions are usually far more interested in what can be grabbed in the way of food and drink, than scanning celebrities for cellulite or prying into their love lives. They are a jolly bunch, usually first with harmless gossip.

Feri Lucas is a Hungarian who has escaped through the Iron Curtain and taken refuge in West London. He is gentle and polite and works as a freelance, selling his work through agencies. His eyes operate like a powerful lens, missing nothing. When he is not in a serious mood they glow with soft warmth.

I am flattered that he wants to take pictures of me. It is his way of getting close to women. He is shy and reserved until he holds a camera in his hand.

He spends an entire day photographing me. He takes me to Richmond Park by bus and persuades me to lie provocatively in some ferns. He photographs me hugging trees, inhaling cigarettes, looking pensive.

Afterwards he gives me a stack of black and white prints that make me look deceptively beautiful. My eyes have grown enormous, my mouth sensual, my hands expressive. I sit in his studio flipping through countless poses. No one has ever given me so much attention. I see myself in an entirely new way. He has drawn 'the hidden' out of me. He has imprisoned me in celluloid and set me free.

He lives in Earls Court in a large room with a high ceiling on the second floor of a Victorian house, in a long, straight road lined by cars. This room serves as living space, studio, and darkroom. The blinds are always down and the centre of the room dominated by photographic lamps and backdrops. The sink and stove are hidden behind a screen - this area doubles as a darkroom. When he is busy developing he puts up a little notice on the screen saying *Do Not Disturb*.

Feri is a perfectionist. His portraits are small masterpieces. His lighting is superb. His skills have been carefully processed over the years.

I go there for dinner sometimes. He gives me green pickled tomatoes and Hungarian wine. I drown in the endless contact sheets he hands me, along with a magnifying glass.

The walls are covered with photographs of countless beautiful women who have been seduced by his lens. He has transformed them into minor goddesses and worships them from a distance. I bring him clients. He takes portraits of Clive. Fran poses topless.

As the months pass unnoticed, Feri's photographs capture the dramatic changes in me. Loss of weight, cheekbones becoming more prominent. Knees sticking out sharply from black tights. Superfluous flesh on my arms disappearing. Eyes darker, much sadder, contentment and sensuousness overshadowed by uncertainty and pain.

My hairstyle changes from shoulder-length to elfin, *Vidal Sassoon* crop, accentuating my sorrow. Mini skirts give way to Mary Quant dresses. Fur jacket is replaced by a black oilskin from *Millet's* with a mandarin collar. Exquisitely tailored, powder blue trouser suit with a short jacket and lined trousers, on which I spend a whole week's wages at *Jaeger*.

I have a pair of white leather ankle boots made by an Indian cobbler in Camden Town. I stand on a piece of cardboard and he draws round my feet to create a pattern. Feri photographs me, wearing these amazing boots and the trouser suit, at night, in brilliantly illuminated doorways in Oxford Street.

Fragment 18: Masochistic Tendencies

THE only photographs ever taken of me and Tony are on our holiday in the Lake District. Because there are so few they are precious. We have neglected the ordinary things couples in love usually do. It has been such a struggle, so dramatic, tempestuous.

Tony shifting from room to room and from mood to mood. I love him however bizarre his behaviour, however depressing the rooms. He finds an old piece of hardboard, paints dots on it, nails it on the wall. He finds a broken typewriter and starts writing a book, typing with one finger.

Sometimes we go to cafés but I am wary now of being verbally abused. He spits out four letter words like bullets, accusing me of crimes I have never committed. I hate it when he becomes paranoid, venting his anger, grabbing me by the sleeve, pushing me out through doors roughly while others drink glasses of coffee that shimmer in the flames of candles stuck in empty wine bottles, and pretend not to hear or see. At such moments I wish I had never set eyes on Tony. My heart racing, my knees weak, terrified of saying something he will misinterpret.

I escape on the Metropolitan Line. Later there will be a call from a pay phone in some rundown house let out in bed-sitters, or one of the kiosks in the entrance to Finchley Road Station. He always apologises and pleads with me to see him again.

How quickly I forget the emotional pain he inflicts. I can only remember that inside the monster is an archangel who lifts me up and carries me away on irresistible, feathery wings.

He'll be calm and gentle for a while, then equilibrium will be lost and another horror movie starts.

During a few sessions of psychoanalysis Mr Barker suggests to me that I have masochistic tendencies.

As a child I had pushed my mother to the limit, retaliating against what I perceived as oppression. Sometimes, if I didn't do as I was told she became angry. I remember cowering. She unwittingly created an emotional ambivalence for I was never quite certain whether I would be treated as child or adult. She played both roles herself, depending on her mood.

Sometimes when I brought Tony home she ignored us both. She often used this blanking technique, addressing other members of the family, as if I wasn't there. An echo of how her mother had sometimes treated her.

As a sensitive adolescent I felt tears pricking behind my eyes like needles. At fourteen, I cried every evening in the cell-like privacy of the upstairs lavatory. I *hated* her then and banged doors.

As I got older she was easier to get on with – *so was I*. Her warm, funny, extrovert side greeted my friends and befriended me. She had a charismatic personality and when she chose could be exceedingly charming.

Maybe if my parents had treated me differently, I would never have fallen in love with Tony? Maybe it wasn't his beautiful face I loved but the perverse nature it masked, the perverse nature that vibrated in harmony with the perversity locked away inside me? Perhaps unconsciously I was excited by these hurricanes because that was the way I had been programmed, with uncertainty. Clive had been mean sometimes. It was sibling rivalry. When we were on the beach on a family holiday he had filled my mouth with sand.

Fragment 19: Saturn in Pisces

MORE than anything else I want Tony to be healed. I still believe it is possible although I don't know how to make it happen.

Analyse and try to understand why. That doesn't seem to work. The emotions, I discover, are much more dominant than the intellect and will. According to Mr Barker changing oneself requires a complete revolution.

Two years earlier when Clive had been struggling with self-doubt before appearing in a movie called *The System,* directed by Michael Winner, Mr Barker had written him the following lines of encouragement.

'You have been much in my mind since your phone call on Friday. I am sure that with your present understanding you will make a great success of the film and this can well be the turning point in your career and life.

You are bound to have occasional troughs of depression and misgiving, but the secret of dealing with them is to see their significance immediately and then to replace the sabotage and the need for exposure with a deep awareness of your essential goodness, your acceptance of yourself and your faith that God and you are working together for fulfilment.

Although I shall not be seeing you, I can assure you that I have a private wire with the Almighty on your behalf and am affirming strongly.'

Mr Barker fully believes in the power of affirmation. Clive responds well. I can't walk away from Tony; forget we'd ever met; harden my heart; be terribly sensible. Why isn't my own life enough? It's a curse needing to fix other people. Why can't I end this charade and concentrate on fixing myself?

Fear surfaces. I push it down with cigarettes, cups of coffee, glasses of wine, food. Fear is always present, warning me. I have no idea what this warning is about so I force it back inside me. It crystallizes into a hard lump. The lump grows more solid and less possible to dissolve. It overshadows my heart. When love tries to bubble up it is blocked.

The fear finds expression when I am followed, or imagine being followed by strangers. My pulse races and my legs go weak. It finds expression in imagining my father dying.

Saturn is passing through my birth sign Pisces when I meet Tony. During the three year transit it turns retrograde for three months, back into his sign, Aquarius. In my birth chart Pisces rules the House of Career, which has certainly been in focus during this time. I read about current planetary influences in an astrology book.

'Saturn is the planet of responsibility and symbolises the ethic of hard work. Under its influence a person's character is strengthened through trial and difficulty. It has been said that Saturn disciplines us until we discipline ourselves.

Are you able to stick with a task until you have completed it? Do you feel beset by problems or see obstacles at every turn? Would other people call you stubborn? Have you sometimes felt lonely and depressed?

If you answer yes, then you have felt the presence of Saturn in your life. The planet is named after the Roman Titan god who was the father of Jupiter, Neptune, and Pluto. Saturn was also a symbol for Father Time, for he brought to an end all things that had a beginning.

In astrology Saturn is the planet of diligence, self-control, and limitation. Its domain is patience, stability, maturity and realism. Its influence is stern and restrictive, cold and severe. In its symbolic form Saturn is our destiny. It rules fate, the things we cannot escape, and the payment we must make for what we receive.'

I know I sometimes receive abundantly from Tony but feel the payment I am expected to make is unfairly high. Have I no control at all? Has everything in my life been already decided by distant planets whirling around in the ether?

I go with Clive to consult Ernest, the astrologer. He has a grey beard and long hair, looks like an engraving by William Blake. He lives in the streets with only a leather coat to protect him from the elements. He carries a holdall full of astrology books wherever he goes.

He draws up charts in a Soho coffee bar in a basement. His voice is drowned by the juke box. He puts up a little cardboard sign with a photograph of Judy Durham of the Australian chart-topping group the Seekers, who has consulted him. He accepts cigarettes as though he is doing something naughty, and always coughs.

He works out my astrological aspects on blue notepaper. He charges five shillings and accepts a cheque.

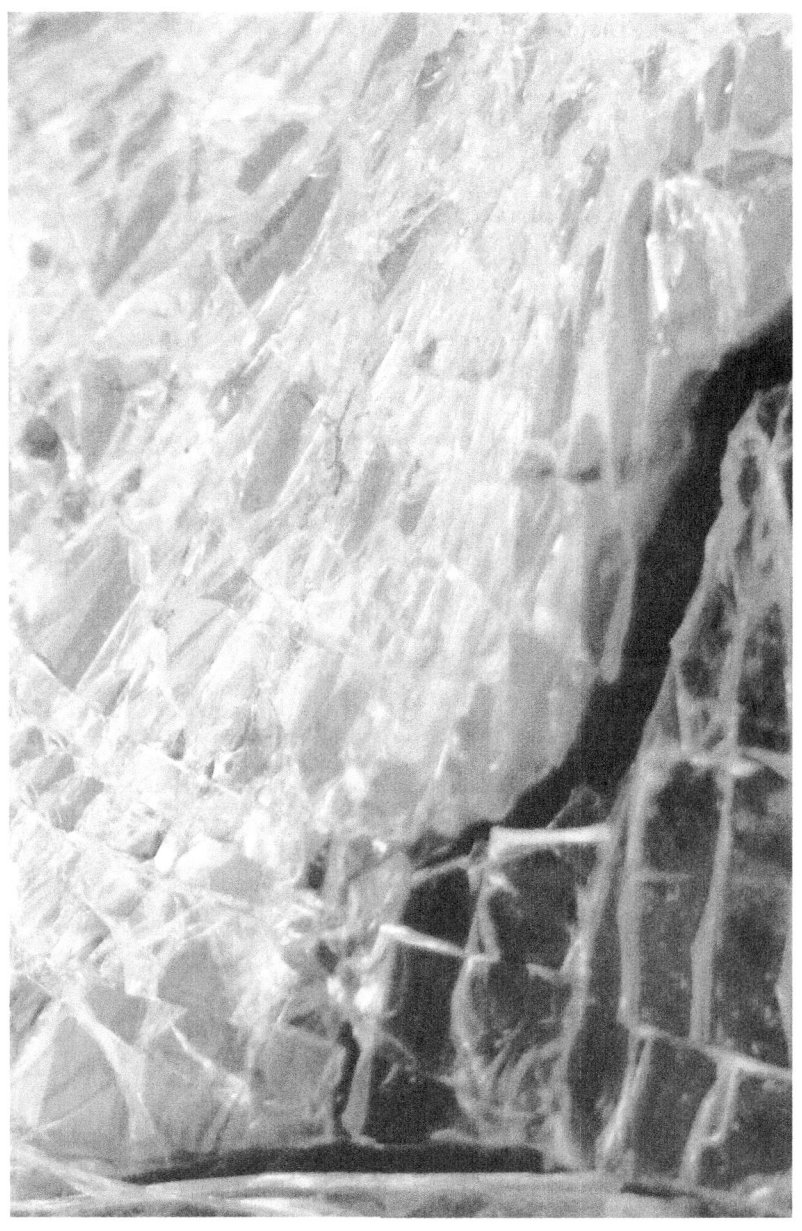

Fragment 20: You're Coming With ME

I am in the middle of a telephone conversation when Tony suddenly appears in my office and pulls the receiver from my hand. This is the first time he has stepped inside the building. When I started working for the magazine I was based in a maze of dingy offices at the back of Regent Street. He had once appeared there from the lift.

Then he had come out of curiosity, and I had been proud of him. He had made quite an impression with his stunning looks. He was wearing a stylish tweed jacket and a grey polo neck sweater. His excuse was that he needed money. I slipped him a pound note, out in the corridor.

But now he is on a different mission. His intent is to get me out, whether I want to leave or not. It is a strange day in so many respects. The planets must be forming extreme aspects.

Two weeks earlier I had left a note on Reg Taylor's desk requesting a raise in salary. If I earned twenty pounds a week I could afford to rent a flat. His response had been slow. I hear nothing from him until this morning when his secretary appears and instructs me to go up to his office. He has obviously been using delaying tactics to unnerve me. It soon becomes obvious that he has no intention of fulfilling my request.

"You appear," he says coldly, "to be working on three cylinders instead of four."

"Well if that's the case," I retort sarcastically, "I must have a cylinder missing."

I return to my desk deciding to play my trump card. While I have been waiting for him to respond I have been offered a job on another magazine, at a much better salary. I have made friends with Michael Aldred, former presenter of the rock/pop TV show *Ready Steady Go!* who introduces me to the editor of *Fabulous.* I have been in two minds about accepting her offer but the matter is now settled.

Gleefully I type out my resignation. I slip it on to Reg Taylor's desk while he is downstairs rowing with Ken. He immediately agrees to pay me twenty pounds, but wishes me every happiness when he realises I have definitely decided to leave.

It is has been quite an eventful morning and now Tony is standing here with a frightening expression in his eyes, commanding me to get my coat.

Yesterday evening I decided I'd had enough. He must have sensed this time I really meant business. I don't know whether I am coming or going because of his odd behaviour. I feel wrecked.

"You're coming with ME," he orders menacingly.

He has hired a taxi and asked the driver to wait so that he can whisk me away. But at this point I know nothing about the taxi. I am simply afraid, desperate to escape. I don't want to be taken prisoner.

The excuse of getting my coat allows me to give him the slip. I fly upstairs into the accounts office.. Tony comes swiftly after me, bounding up the stairs, two at a time. He pounces on me like prey, grabbing my hair and arm, dragging me screaming.

The women in Accounts are in shock. I feel myself being bumped downstairs, a limp rag doll. People rise from their desks when they hear the commotion.

Only Ken in his silence continues to work.

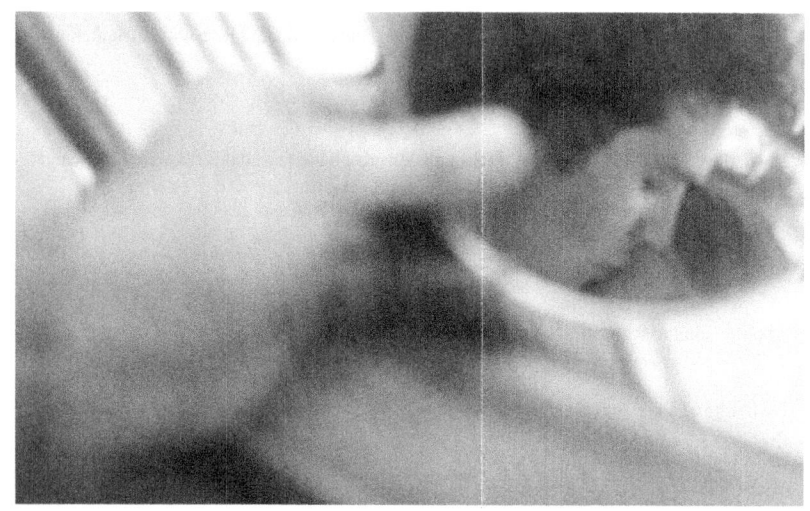

Fragment 21: Broken Glass

IT is fortunate that earlier I resolved things with Reg Taylor who is now outside on the grey Mayfair pavements surrounded by a crowd, demonstrating his judo skills, perfected as a commando in the Navy.

Tony towers over him but he nimbly pins his arm behind his back and forces him inside again. It is extraordinary how easily he seems to deal with the situation. He pushes Tony up two flights of stairs to his plush office, where they hold board meetings, and closes the door while he delivers a fatherly lecture.

A few minutes later he returns Tony to my office, *to talk things through calmly.* Reg Taylor assumes this is merely a lovers' quarrel that has flared out of control. He sees it like a discarded cigarette end accidentally starting an explosion. He feels pleased with himself. He lost face when I resigned but has regained his position, and undoubtedly impressed his staff too.

For the second time that day he is mistaken. What am I supposed to say after my boyfriend has created such a scene? Does he really imagine we are going to walk down Oxford Street hand in hand?

I am frozen. Tony moves towards my desk, picks up my heavy manual typewriter. For a split second I think he is going to throw it at me. I flinch. But he aims at the large bay window and hurls it through the glass that splinters all over the office. The typewriter lands like a bomb, in a mangled heap behind a hairdressing salon.

I move away warily. I can't bear to look at him. Vicky Charlton, the journalist who shares the office, is traumatised. Afterwards, she claims he crawled on his knees and tried to eat the glass. I know she is exaggerating. He is not *that* crazy.

Now I am jolting through the London traffic in a Black Maria. Reg Taylor with his corduroy trilby on his knees is sitting opposite. Tony is handcuffed and flanked by two police officers. He is crying like a small boy. I long to lean across to comfort him.

Reg Taylor is furious when he discovers I intend to intervene. He warns me not to interfere. He is there to make a statement about damaged property and is only interested in compensation.

The court clerk tells me it will help a great deal if I explain clearly, in my statement, all that has happened. I gaze down at the sheet of lined foolscap as if I am about to sit an important exam.

Tony is charged with assaulting me and damaging property. I try to see the positive side. I hope this crisis will draw attention to his problems.

They lock him in a cell overnight and I am secretly glad.

Fragment 22: A Month In Prison

TONY is sent to prison for a month. He is ordered to pay compensation for the damage and bound over not to contact me.

I am devastated. My statement is completely ignored by the magistrate.

Friends rally round. Jim Ramble enjoys the drama and takes me under his wing. We play Otis Reading's *My Girl* and smoke some hash. I am hurt and damaged.

The drama is splashed all over the papers. I who have written the news suddenly become the news and this feels extremely uncomfortable. I slam down the phone on journalists who want an exclusive. The incident is hot gossip in pop circles.

'*LOVESICK SWAIN GOES TO JAIL*'. I read the headlines in a daze and feel detached, as if nothing is real.

I took a long time writing my statement, explained that you were ill and needed help, not punishment. I was relieved you were locked up in a cell. No door in my body was strong enough to keep you out.

Your bruised emotions were weapons turned out towards me. Making me appear responsible for wounds I had not inflicted, only uncovered. Making me scared to be myself in case I accidentally slipped out of the part you had invented. Making my life as painful as yours, then weeping at the horror you had created and begging my forgiveness.

And then I had dominance because of your weakness. I would grow less generous and gradually exploit my new power. I would expect more than meekness, more than being a mother to a naughty child who needed her to exist. My desires unleashed the fury in you and I became the child again, cowering, waiting and willing you to hurt me so that again I could condemn you.

And so we swung as on trapezes, sometimes holding hands in the middle and finding each other for a moment.

And because Tony is physically stronger and because his emotions are out of control, he is sick, dangerous. Whereas I am confused, and harmful only to myself.

He came into court, a saint in a grey jumper with holes in. He followed a drunk and a Black guy who had stolen rolls of cloth, who is discharged despite fourteen previous convictions.

Tony stood there. Gazed around bewildered.

HOLY IS THE EXTREMIST WHO PURSUES HOLINESS. THEREFORE I WORSHIPPED YOU. YOUR BODY THE ALTAR I PLACED MYSELF UPON. I ANOINTED YOU. I SAW STIGMATA IN YOUR HANDS AND A GASH IN YOUR SIDE WHERE SOMEONE HAD TRIED TO STEAL YOUR HEART. I SAW YOU WITH THORNS, AND BLOOD IN YOUR EYES RAISED TO HEAVEN. PEOPLE MOCKED AND SPAT AT YOU WHILE YOU HUNG HELPLESS. YOU WERE THE ONLY SAVIOUR I COULD SEE.

I TOOK YOU DOWN FROM YOUR CROSS AND WRAPPED YOU IN A FINE, PERFUMED GARMENT. ALTHOUGH YOU WERE DEAD YOU WERE STILL WARM AND HEAVY. AND I CARRIED YOU AROUND WITH ME.

Somehow I get on with my work and my life. The local newspaper devotes the whole of the front page to the story. My mother hides it, scared of upsetting me even more. But I am not content to leave things alone. I desire more than anything that Tony should be given treatment. I can't accept that we live in a society where people can climb to an emotional precipice and be allowed to jump over the edge.

I resolve never to see him again but believe it is possible to help him somewhere in the background.

Clive is supportive, although he doesn't really like Tony. He stresses that I would not be to blame if Tony took his own life. The thought has never even occurred to me. He agrees to go with me to Brixton Prison to see the welfare officer.

Clive wears a short dark overcoat and tight black trousers, slightly flared. He gets a kick out of the part. We are both dangerous idealists.

The prison visit is a complete waste of time. The welfare officer seems only interested in establishing Tony's sexual orientation. He wants to know who will deal with the practicalities when he gets home. I wonder where home is. By now his possessions have probably been dumped beside dustbins, along with his rent book.

Tony writes to me on prison notepaper, wishing me happy birthday, saying how much he misses seeing the sky. He says there are others in there, far worse off than him.

Fragment 23: A New Job

MY new job on *Fabulous* takes me to a vast office block at the end of Fleet Street. I travel on packed trains to Blackfriars Station. I feel like an open wound that needs stitching. Somehow I manage to keep going, improvise, try not to think of Tony.

I quickly realise this is a totally alien way of working. The editor, Unity Hall, charming and approachable at my interview, has become distant now I am member of staff. She is in her early thirties, an experienced and hardened newspaper woman. She calls me into her office to point out spelling mistakes in my copy.

"You haven't done your homework. Have you ducky?"

I am becoming nervous of her. It's like being back at school. I discover that the magazine has a strict policy, dictated by Unity. Individuality is frowned upon. I am expected to write to a formula, which I find extremely difficult. The magazine presents a false, glossy impression of the pop scene for its teenage readers.

The extraordinary thing is that it involves so many editorial meetings to produce this magazine. My creativity normally flows easily, but I find it hard to think of silly ideas for features. I sit behind my typewriter, having panic attacks, unable to meet deadlines because my mind is frozen.

The assistant editor has worked her way up to this illustrious position over the years, starting off as a lift girl. I share an office with one of Unity's favourites, who churns out endless perfectly spelt and presented copy. Each comma, question mark, and adjective falls in exactly the right place.

For the first time since I entered journalism, I doubt my abilities. Everyone must be at their desk by 9.30 precisely.

I begin to realise I am not a good time-keeper. I have never watched clocks. I have sat at desks until late in the evening and never counted the number of hours I work. I give of my time freely, especially if I enjoy what I am doing. Now if I am one second late I have to report to Unity.

Unity decides to move all the staff – subs, graphic artists, frantically busy feature writers - into one huge office so that she has more control. She invents a nerve-wracking system. A buzzer is installed on her desk and wired through to this office. Each member of staff is given a number. When Unity buzzes a particular number of times, whoever owns it must immediately drop everything and hasten to her side. The buzzer is harsh and intrusive. I sit at my desk, struggling for inspiration, waiting to spring up instantly at the sound of the dreaded six buzzes that summon me.

I am allocated the fashion spread and the gossip page at the front of the magazine. I am also expected to produce several features each week on pop stars.

I tour a farm with the iconic mod group the Small Faces, accompanied by a photographer. Instead of a straight interview about their music and personal life, I have bizarrely to report about how they go into pigsties and s*nort!*

'They frequently catch sight of the countryside, but that's when dawn's coming up over a motorway and they're just far too sleepy to appreciate Nature's handiwork. Therefore a day out on a farm with the breeze ruffling their hair and bringing colour to their pale cheeks was considered a gas sort of idea by the Small Faces. At Cottage Farm, Potters

Bar, we were greeted by our host for the day, farmer Mr Ensten. He was plodding around happily in the mud in Wellington boots.

Steve Marriot leaps into the farmhouse kitchen to change into old gear. He was very determined to get dirty. Getting dirty didn't take a long time, or much effort because the farm is home to 400 pigs of all shapes, sizes, and snorts! And pigs as you know are extremely fond of mud, especially rolling around in it.

The boys ran over to the nearest sty. They remembered boys at school who looked like pigs!

"Got very bad manners that one," Stevie said pointing to one porker which was snuffling about and poking its nose in the air and grunting.

"Look at their hairy ears," laughed Mac.

"Yeh," said Stevie. "And their weird boat-races. He looks so sad that one. They all look sad 'cos all of 'em have little minces!" '

I have to conjure up 2,000 words of pigs' swill. I will never forget the disgust with which I wrote the article or how cold and muddy the farm was.

'We'd all had a great time. And it must have been an unforgettable day for the farm animals too, especially the pigs. Because Stevie had said, "I dig pigs!" It's not often a gorgeous boy says a flattering thing like that to a pig!'

This issue of the magazine also contains a black and white portrait of a rather ordinary looking musician with a Caesar haircut. I am instructed to write a whole page on why he is the possible Face of '66. After hours of thought I begin: '*There is something about his brow that recalls the nobleman of Ancient Rome...*'

I enjoy dining at the Pickwick Club with American singer Gene Pitney and some of our readers who have won a competition. Gene is unusually pleasant and unassuming for such a big star. Rock band Dave Dee, Dozy, Beaky, Mick and Tich invade the office for a photo shoot. One of them pulls off his boots and has such smelly feet that we have to fling open all the windows!

The manager of the Troggs wants my opinion on their hot new single. He plays the demo over the phone. I am the first journalist to hear the exciting *Wild Thing!* It pulses from the receiver into my body.

After a month's respite from Tony I still miss him. I wake up in the middle of the night from dreams where we have been making love. My body is perpetually in a semi-aroused state because of the way I feel about him. We are linked together by invisible emotions and inescapable telepathy. We are tangled up in each other's auras because we have made love so many times.

I never feel out of his reach.

On the day he is released he phones begging to see me in a few months, if he straightens himself out. I try to sharpen my voice, to kill the frail hope that limps between us.

AFTER A WHILE I PULLED OFF THE MASK OF MY RESISTANCE AND HELD IT IN MY HANDS SURE THAT THE FACE STARING BACK AT ME WAS NOT MINE. IT WAS A FACE THAT ATTEMPTED ONLY TO CONCEAL. I AGREED TO

MEET YOU, YOU SOUNDED SO DESPERATE. I MISTOOK THE DRAMA OF LOSS FOR THAT OF LOVE. IT WAS EASIER TO FEEL SOMETHING WHEN SOMEONE ELSE WAS CRYING.

I regret my decision as soon as I see him. His hair has been shorn. There is a trapped expression in his eyes. We go to a café expanded by mirrors, and he keeps standing up and gazing at himself, to make sure he is still there.

He gives me three narrow, metal bracelets the colours of the sky and I put them on like handcuffs.

We rent an enormous room for the night, overwhelmed by floorboards and furniture. He trembles in my arms.

He is lost next morning, trying to make conversation with people at a long table, crunching toast and marmalade. He goes to change some money to pay the bill and I hear him singing in the street.

YET I IMAGINED FREEDOM ONLY AS A CHANCE TO RUN AWAY. AND SO OUR LOVE DANCED BEFORE ME, A CLOWN IN WHOSE CHANGING EXPRESSION I ALWAYS MANAGED TO DEFEAT MYSELF.

I have lost confidence in the relationship. I am afraid. I refuse to see him again and imagine him lurking around everywhere, waiting to pounce on me. I am afraid he will be waiting at Blackfriars Station, or outside the office. I am afraid of myself, afraid of everything.

Unity Hall instructs the switchboard to monitor all my calls, when I explain Tony won't stop phoning. She gives me a lecture about being more sensible in my choice of friends. I hate drawing attention to myself in this way and feel humiliated. I even suspect innocent men of stalking me.

RECREATING AN EXCITEMENT I UNCONSCIOUSLY DESIRE. LOST YOU AND STILL WANTING YOU AT THE CORE OF MY BEING. PROJECTING YOUR IMAGE ON TO THE BLANK SCREENS OF STRANGERS. FEARING THEM INSTEAD.

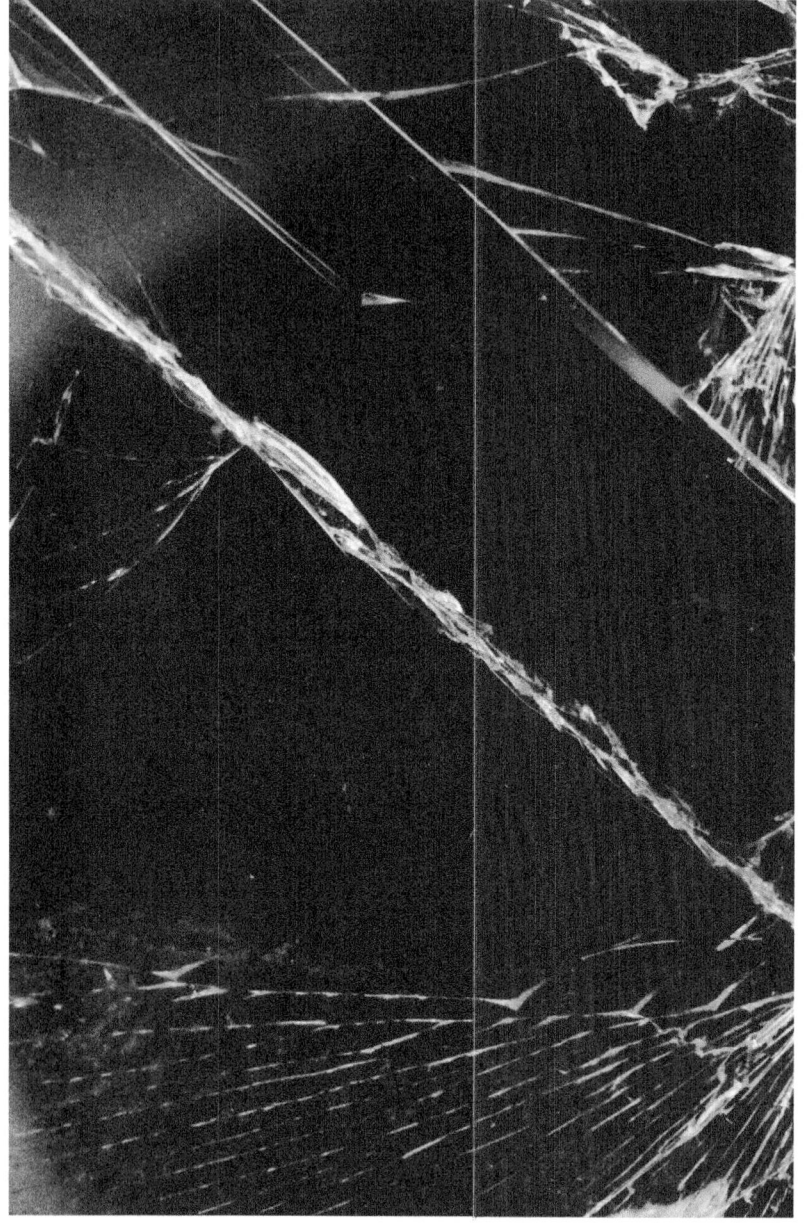

Fragment 24: A Bird That Refuses To Learn That Glass Is Impenetrable

THE only friend I make while working at *Fabulous* appears at my office one spring morning. Artist Barry Fantoni is promoting his single *Little Man In A Little Box*. He is also a presenter on *A Whole Scene Going*, the BBC's culture show for teenagers.

He invites me to his flat at Clapham Common. It is on the ground floor and has huge, shuttered windows. Barry uses the room overlooking the common as a studio. There is a grand piano, shelves crammed with books, stuffed birds in glass cases, dinky toys.

I am impressed by his dedication and professionalism. He is either painting a front cover for one of the Sunday supplements, dreaming up jokes for *Private Eye*, composing a song, or working on his portrait of the great stand-up comic Max Miller. He glues a real pearl on Max's tie on which he has painted a parrot.

Because he is an artist he puts me into perspective. The flat smells of oil paint, turpentine, and Edwardian leather chairs. He makes me laugh. I don't feel I have been allowed to laugh for a long time. I feel lighter because of his sense of fun and outrageousness.

Tony is still heavily on my mind. He is due to appear in court again because my parents have persuaded me to report that he has broken the conditions of his bind over. I can't face going to court. I write to the clerk saying I am ill and ask for the case to be adjourned for a month. I am hoping to find someone who will represent Tony. I try organisations for helping people who are mentally ill. They are either too busy or tell me not to interfere. I can't accept that our fate is irrevocable, our destiny out of my control.

Eventually the dreaded day dawns and Tony strides into court wearing plimsolls without socks. My heart flies out to him, a bird which foolishly refuses to learn that glass is impenetrable, that the sky is only as high as you can fly.

I dash outside, unwilling to face my decision. My parents tell me to behave like an adult. I go back into the court and sit down. I look into his eyes. He grins and sticks his tongue out. I grin back. We are accused of acting like children. We're innocent. We don't want to play this horrible game.

I tell the magistrate all I know about Tony. I explain he needs help. He replies that in cases of mental illness the court is powerless.

Tony is growing angry as he stands on trial. He says he is a poet and earns a few shillings taking a dog for a walk. I heard the dog barking the day he phoned pleading with me to drop the case. He shouted at the dog because he couldn't hear what I was saying.

They fine him £25 and bind him over for a long period. He is warned that if he bothers me again he will be immediately arrested.

WE WALK OUT OF SEPARATE DOORS AND INTO SEPARATE LIVES, WITH EACH OTHER INSIDE US.

Fragment 25: Cheese And Biscuits

I interview Terry Stamp at his flat in the Albany, Piccadilly. He agrees to appear in an issue of *Fabulou*s entitled *Gorgeous Men.* When I arrive he has just been riding and is polishing a pair of elegant riding boots.

The Collector in which Terry brilliantly plays a psychopath, who collects butterflies and then women, has recently been released. I saw it at a cinema in Leicester Square.

He offers me cheese and biscuits and a glass of red wine, and we sit on the floor chatting. I tell him about Tony and what has happened. I am still hurting from the court appearance. He talks about his girlfriend, Jean Shrimpton, the supermodel.

I leave on a high, floating along Piccadilly. He has made me feel that all things are possible.

My dislike of working for *Fabulous* doesn't go away. I hate being stuck in an office with so many industrious, intimidated people.

One grey afternoon is brightened up by Twiggy with her manager-boyfriend Justin de Villeneuve. We do the interview in a new doughnut bar at the bottom of Fleet Street. Twiggy giggles infectiously and devours an enormous number of doughnuts.

Fragment 26: Dylan

THINGS seem to be looking up when I am invited to a press conference for Bob Dylan at the Mayfair Hotel in Park Lane. Dylan is my idol and the fact that I am about to see him in the flesh compensates for everything.

I find myself in a large room packed with journalists. Dylan is sitting at a table wearing shades. The Press are grilling him.

I stand at the back of the room absorbing the atmosphere, irritated by the mocking questions. But Dylan is giving as good as he gets, cutting through the fear with intelligence and inspiration.

I feel I am at a celestial gathering. Dylan is at the centre of power, generating golden light.

I am wearing a sleeveless cream dress with a round neck. It is short and fine. My body seems fleshless. My suffering has transformed me. I consist of jangling emotions weighted down by the lightest skin and bone. I am almost ethereal.

I try to imagine Dylan's eyes behind the black lenses. I smile at his clever retorts. Why do these journalists want to crucify him? I suppose he emphasises their shallowness and dishonesty. He is spotlighting their doubt. I am not one of them. I have defected to Dylan's side, but not bold enough to speak.

The crowd around Dylan is disintegrating. The vultures have feasted.

I stand there hesitating when a macho American, wearing a floral shirt and white shoes, approaches. He is part of Dylan's entourage. "Dylan digs you," he tells me and I find myself being escorted through the maze of hotel corridors. So I didn't imagine it. I sensed, despite the shades, that he has been looking directly at me, knew what I was feeling.

POET AND MUSICIAN WITH MUSIC WORDS AND MUSIC THAT SPEAKS LIKE A FIELD OF VAN GOGH'S FLOWERS. SOFT SUEDE JACKET AND GOBLIN SHOES AND TROUSERS WITH STRIPES. MYSTERY BEHIND YOUR DARK GLASSES THAT ATTEMPT TO HIDE YOUR ANCIENT, DEAD, YOUNG, ALIVE EYES.

Quite astonishingly I am now outside my idol's suite. Dylan appears. He seems smaller and frailer, and is still wearing the shades. All kinds of thoughts are rushing through my head. There is so much I want to say to him.

I persuade him to remove his dark glasses. I desperately want to look into his eyes. He giggles and gives in, flicking them off and revealing himself.

I can't believe this is happening. It's like a dream.

He wants me to come inside. I imagine an incredible scene behind the door. But panic surfaces as I remember the existence of Unity Hall and her instructions about being back in the office immediately after lunch.

"I've got a deadline to meet. Look I'll come back later." I can't believe I just said *that*. I could strangle myself.

Dylan tells me the extension to ask for and disappears, replacing the disguise. I am so elated that it takes some time for the fact that I have blown it, to really sink in. Later I call the hotel, and Dylan's line is permanently engaged.

When I wake up next morning I discover Clive has pinned up a large black and white poster of Dylan on my bedroom wall. It is a shot of him *without s*hades.

My friend Hugh Nolan, a journalist I worked with on the Weekly Post in Ickenham, is now a feature writer on the music paper *Disc*. He phones me to tell me he has two tickets for the Dylan concert at the Royal Albert Hall.

When I first met Hugh he appeared dead straight. He had married in his teens and had a little boy. Now he has grown his hair into a halo of curls, and gone hippy.

We climb the steps outside the Royal Albert Hall with hundreds of devoted fans. Hugh thrusts a joint into my hand and by the time we reach the auditorium this dark womb is Heaven. Angels light candles. Hugh flicks open his gold lighter and is in spasms of ecstasy beside me. Dylan has gone electric and seems stoned.

A few days after I meet Dylan, I wake up in the middle of the night and come to the conclusion that all journalists are parasites. I want to do something creative, not feed off creative people. And more than anything I am angry with myself for being dominated by my fear of Unity Hall. I feel I have let myself down badly, rejecting Dylan's invitation, betraying everything I claim to believe in.

I act swiftly and decisively. I hand in my resignation.

FOLLOW HIM THROUGH THE SCENTED CLOUDS THAT WILL HARM ONLY THE UNSEEING AND THOSE WHO HAVE NOTHING ELSE. FOLLOW HIM, CLINGING ON TO HIS HEARTBEATS.

Fragment 27: There Are Moments That Shock Me

I relinquish my job at *Fabulous* with much more ease than I give up Tony. The latter has been forced upon me. I accept it like punishment.

For a few weeks I am in a vacuum with nothing to do. Feri continues to capture my sadness in a stream of black and white prints - then Ken offers me freelance work. I work at home in my bedroom with Dylan staring down at me. Ken teaches me the art of writing short stories.

"Just think of a title," he instructs, "and base the story on that."

I find this technique effective and begin churning out love stories. *Warm Girl On The Coldest Day, Strawberry Love, When The Bus Stop Turned To Gold.*

For the first time ever I can organise my own time. I can stay in bed late, work when I want - no one but myself to answer to. I invest in a portable typewriter, an Olivetti Lettera 32, and this, plus a few sheets of blank paper, are all I need to make a living.

I go to Ken's office regularly and we always end up in the Marlborough Head on the corner of North Audley Street, discussing story ideas. Ken is going through a long, slow crisis. He is still mourning his son. Sometimes he stumbles because of lack of balance caused by his deafness. Today he has a plaster on his forehead. He collapsed on the metal-capped steps down to the tube. When he was wounded in the war his lungs were damaged by shrapnel.

Our mutual pain draws us together. Our relationship is platonic. He shows how he feels in his eyes, by the way he gets up and moves towards the bar to buy me a drink, as soon as I enter the pub. He is as pleased to see me as a puppy.

"Am I shouting?" he whispers. He once asked me if they still ring bells at closing time.

Ken gives me all that my father has never given me. He regards me as a daughter. He feels responsible for me. He pumps confidence into me with his promises of more work.

Reg Taylor is putting pressure on him. *Boyfriend*, not long ago the most popular on the scene, is losing circulation. New magazines are being launched to meet the growing demands of teenagers. Ken gives the magazine a make-over, changes the title to *Trend*.

The weather grows warmer. The love stories flow and I miss Tony. My less demanding lifestyle forces me to look at myself more closely and I lapse into depression.

I go to Barry's flat for a cup of tea. I catch the tube to Clapham Common, pass the little shops, stroll along South Side under the high trees. In the autumn the dead leaves rattle, and a circus arrives.

I am wearing white trousers and a pink, white, and brown top with horizontal stripes. My flat, pink and white shoes have laces and peep toes. I am coming out of mourning, beginning to free myself.

Tony knows I have interviewed Barry and finds his address in the telephone directory. He sends me a letter c/o South Side.

'I keep hoping to see you step into places where I am but never do. I see a girl who looks like you but it's only someone else. I haven't been doing anything special lately. I went

to Spain earlier in the year, roaming and everything. Then I came back to England for two months. Then I went off again only to return.

I have been trying to think of ways of making a bit of money. I have been itching to do a really souped up version of Romeo and Juliet with motorbikes and glass being smashed everywhere.'

There is a c/o address for me to reply.

Another letter comes which begins, *'You RAT for not writing to me...'*

Early one evening I drive to Hampstead with my mother for a meditation session with an India guru who sits cross-legged on the floor and radiates saffron. Afterwards I decide to catch the tube. My mother drops me off in the street and drives away.

I walk straight into Tony. There is no way I could have avoided him. He invites me to a coffee bar. The pavement goes soft beneath my feet. My voice trembles as I grope for words that will calm but no hurt his feelings or give him hope. I can sense his bottled-up emotions, like wild beasts on the verge of stampeding.

Tony sends another letter c/o Barry.

'HELLO, I wished I could have spoken to you for a lot longer. There was a lot more that I could say. I still love you ever so much. I haven't loved anyone before. It's just you forever I suppose. As for our seeing each other again that's something I'd be very afraid of because of the awful things I begin to do.

There are moments that shock me. Instances when you've said something or other times. It's been my own fault. But it's difficult because of what I feel about you.

I am trying to sort out my physical self. I try to eat only the best sort of food and absolutely no smoking. People are very stupid and some of the things they do. I am trying not to be. Living is for the senses as well as the mind. Oh Jesus I want to make love to you. If only you knew how much. Come back to me. Give me another chance. If you do consider this at all let's meet somewhere 'cos I can't write it all, can I? But I do love you, so at least there is that.

So at least give me another chance to see you, to discuss. I might not see you all next year.' The letter makes me bleed.

AND MY HEART IS MADE OF GLASS AND BREAKS. AND I MEND MY HEART MYSELF.

Fragment 28: A New Life

I play Dylan's *Positively Fourth Street*, over and over again in my bedroom as I work on the portable typewriter. The clatter of the keys and his grating voice blend.

The raw energy in Dylan's music charges me. I feel as if I'm not entirely alone.

My mother, because of her own unresolved emotional issues, has over the years, dabbled in various therapies. She advises me to have some sessions with a hypnotherapist.

"You have started a new life," Mr Stocker tells me. I'm not convinced. Ken says I'm refusing to put Tony away, like an old teddy bear.

"You have started a new life."

The light filters through white Venetian blinds in the hypnotherapist's office. He tells me to fix my gaze on the lamp hanging from the ceiling.

"It will be a very pleasant feeling. All the nerves and muscles in your body relaxing, relaxing. You will go on from day to day more positively, one thing after another, taking an interest in everything you do.

There are millions and millions of people in the world, a number too great for any of us to imagine. Many of these people suffer from anxieties or fears, have bad nerves as we say.

A man came to me the other day who felt as if he had a metal band round his head. Had he been physically examined his head would have been quite normal.

A woman came to me. She said she felt as if she was falling to pieces. Of course many of us often feel like this when we can't cope.

There are millions and millions of people in the world, a number too great for you to comprehend.

You will be able to cope. You will feel much better. And when I count to five you will gradually rouse yourself. You will feel more relaxed, more composed. You will have more ability to cope with situations you have lost confidence to handle.

ONE - TWO - THREE - FOUR - FIVE. Because your friend got out of control it doesn't mean this is likely to happen again. You are beginning a new life."

I repeat to myself, "I have begun a new life without you."

Fragment 29: Escape

MY mother is taking a drug call Librium. It makes her feel tranquil. It makes her forget all losses, disappointments, frustrations and fear.

Tranquillisers are considered a wonder drug. The generally held belief is emerging that it is no longer necessary to cope with grief or anxiety because a little pill will soothe them away. But nobody realises they are addictive and have nasty side effects. From now on my mother will be trapped on prescribed drugs that are as difficult to kick as cocaine and heroin. As far back as I can remember she has also taken sleeping pills.

Clive has difficulty sleeping too and my mother often slips him a few of her pills. He gets prescriptions of amphetamines from the family doctor. His breakdown has faded into the background. He is still living with Fran in Chelsea. His close relationship with her appears to have sorted out most of his problems. He has given up therapy with Mr Barker. It is expensive and anyway they have fallen out because of Mr Barker's attitude over what he regards as Clive's lack of self-discipline.

I smoke joints with my friends. Smoking makes things happen more spontaneously. There is no future. It appears easier to get much closer to people.

Since 1964 Saturn has been transiting Pisces and continues to do so until spring 1967 when the drug culture peaks. Pisces is the sign of self-undoing, confusion, prompts overindulgence in drugs and alcohol. Pisces yearns to escape into psychedelic dreams.

Fragment 30: The Circle Line

LATE one afternoon in the early autumn, I push my way on to a train on the Circle Line. I peer down through the straphangers, spot one empty seat at the end of the carriage. Tony is sitting in the next seat. I make my way along the carriage as if pulled by a string. I wish I could control the elation that swells up inside me. It is months since I saw him. We have both changed.

He is calm and sun-tanned but underneath the black, rolled neck sweater his heart is breaking open too. He smiles radiantly, as if everything is now all right.

It is inevitable that we will alight on the platform together. As far as I am concerned this meeting is predestined. Neither of us can be blamed for this overpowering, magnetic attraction.

Before I can think straight I am beside him naked, in yet another Hampstead bed-sitter.

I am beyond hope, skinny from not eating regularly and smoking too much.

He has pulled the mattress on to the floor and piled up all the ugly, heavy furniture in a small mountain at the back of the room. The room is sunny, better than many others. There are tall trees outside the bay window and in them birds sing.

A dusty mirror is propped up over the fireplace. Some days later, I write *I LOVE YOU* in the dust with my index finger.

If only I had caught a different train.

Fragment 31: Between The Broken Glass The People Play

A thoughtless remark accidentally flies out of my mouth like a spear. Tony is wounded. He grabs hold of me and bangs my head against the wall. He has no control over his temper. He is full of remorse. He bangs his fist against the wall and the entire world shudders.

He picks up the mirror on which I had written *I LOVE YOU* and hurls it through the window into the street. He works his way through the mountain of second-hand furniture - wardrobe, bedstead, chest of drawers, armchairs, all hurtling through the air. The ultimate and most terrifying temper tantrum.

WHY DID YOU HAVE TO SMASH ALL THIS? WHY DID YOU BREAK ALL THIS? YOU SHATTERED A WORLD INSIDE MY HEAD AND BANGED ME UP AGAINST THE WALL UNTIL I SAW RAINBOWS AND FELT ONLY FEAR.

YOU HIT ME AS IF I WAS AN ENEMY. YOU HATED ME, FOR GRADUALLY YOU KNEW YOU WERE MY MURDERER, AND YOUR OWN.

AND YOU FELL AGAINST ME AND CRIED SUCH TERRIBLE HOT TEARS. I CRIED TOO, FROM SHOCK. OUR TEARS WERE DIFFERENT.

HEAVEN AND EARTH WAS BEING BROKEN, ALL THE WINDOWS. DREAMS.

THERE WAS A GIRL IN THE BATHROOM WASHING. WE CLUNG TOGETHER IN THE DARKNESS. AND WHEN YOU HAD FINISHED YOUR SMASHING YOU CALLED FOR ME AND I RAN WITH YOU.

I WAS FRIGHTENED ON THAT TRAIN. AND YOU, YOU WERE MARVELLING AT THE LIGHTS ON THE RIVER, AS IT PULLED OUT TAKING US NOWHERE.

NOW YOU HAVE SMASHED EVERYTHING, WHILE BETWEEN THE BROKEN GLASS THE PEOPLE PLAY.

Fragment 32: Panic

TONY stands at the end of Glenloch Road, Hampstead in the twilight and waves on the police car that speeds in the direction of the house where he has created such chaos. He has forced me to leave with him. I am trembling with shock and amazed at his audacity, his apparent lack of remorse. He behaves as if he is on a film set. I know there is no point in pinching myself. I am *never* going to wake up.

We catch a tube to a main line station - I cannot remember which one - and then take a train to somewhere on the other side of the Thames. I don't remember the name of the place.

We stay the night at the home of Tony's cousin. He opens the door in his dressing gown, frowning. I am forced to share the sofa with Tony and feel simultaneously vulnerable and numb.

I am trying to pacify him. I smile nervously and make all sorts of promises I never intend to keep. I am more frightened of him now than I have ever been before. He has finally shattered all my illusions.

Fortunately he has never been really violent to me. He hasn't punched me or blacked my eyes. Surprisingly even though he has slapped me hard around the face on occasions, he has never left marks. He lashes out in frustration. He is like a gas-filled room when a match is accidentally struck.

Somehow, I manage to get free. I can't recall his plans. I doubt he had any. He can't return to the smashed room, any more than we can return to the shelter of our hopelessly damaged affair. The phone calls start early in the morning. Tony rings and rings but hangs up when my father answers. The only person I feel able to confide in is Barry. I sit in the ecclesiastical calm of his studio and confess my sins, while he works on a caricature of Melvyn Bragg.

"Leave the country," he advises, somewhat dramatically.

I get up early, fold my clothes in a white vinyl suitcase, creep out of the house. I catch the underground to Victoria but when I arrive I am too nervous to go to the ticket office. I am afraid Tony has read my mind, knows my plans, will be waiting to stop me.

Instead of passing under the huge clock where I have met so many friends, I step outside, hail a cab. I travel all the way to Gatwick. It costs £5 but I feel the expense is justified. I already have a plane ticket to Jersey and £20 in cash. I know no one at all on the island. Ken, who is aware of my sudden departure, has promised to accept short stories from me, if I can manage to write.

When I arrive in Jersey I take another cab to one of the most exclusive hotels on the island, *La Pomme D'Or*. I once went there for afternoon tea when I was on holiday. I can't think of anywhere else to go.

My composure in such unpredictable circumstances is somewhat miraculous. I am being propelled by a power outside of myself. At breakfast the immaculately attired waiter treats me politely when I ask for more fruit juice.

I go to an employment agency and am advised to find a job as a nanny. I hire another car to take me through the winding lanes to an elegant, Spanish style farmhouse where I am greeted by a housekeeper in a uniform and shown into a magnificent kitchen.

The owner of this awesome property is a woman with a heavily lined face and American accent.

She explains that her daughter needs help with her two small children. Her daughter and son-in-law arrive and soon I am being driven through the Jersey countryside to their apartment. My white suitcase and portable typewriter are in the boot. I feel like a vagrant.

Tony and I walking in Maida Vale one Saturday evening noticed an old tramp sitting in a bus shelter with a little pram. He was wearing a shabby, discoloured mackintosh and a hat with flaps. I felt sorry for him in the windy shelter and decided to ask him back to the flat in Warwick Avenue for the night.

He accepted, somewhat suspiciously, trailing behind. I recall the squeaking pram packed with provisions and the stars shining high above in the ice-cold sky. Ironically, how warm and secure I felt beside Tony.

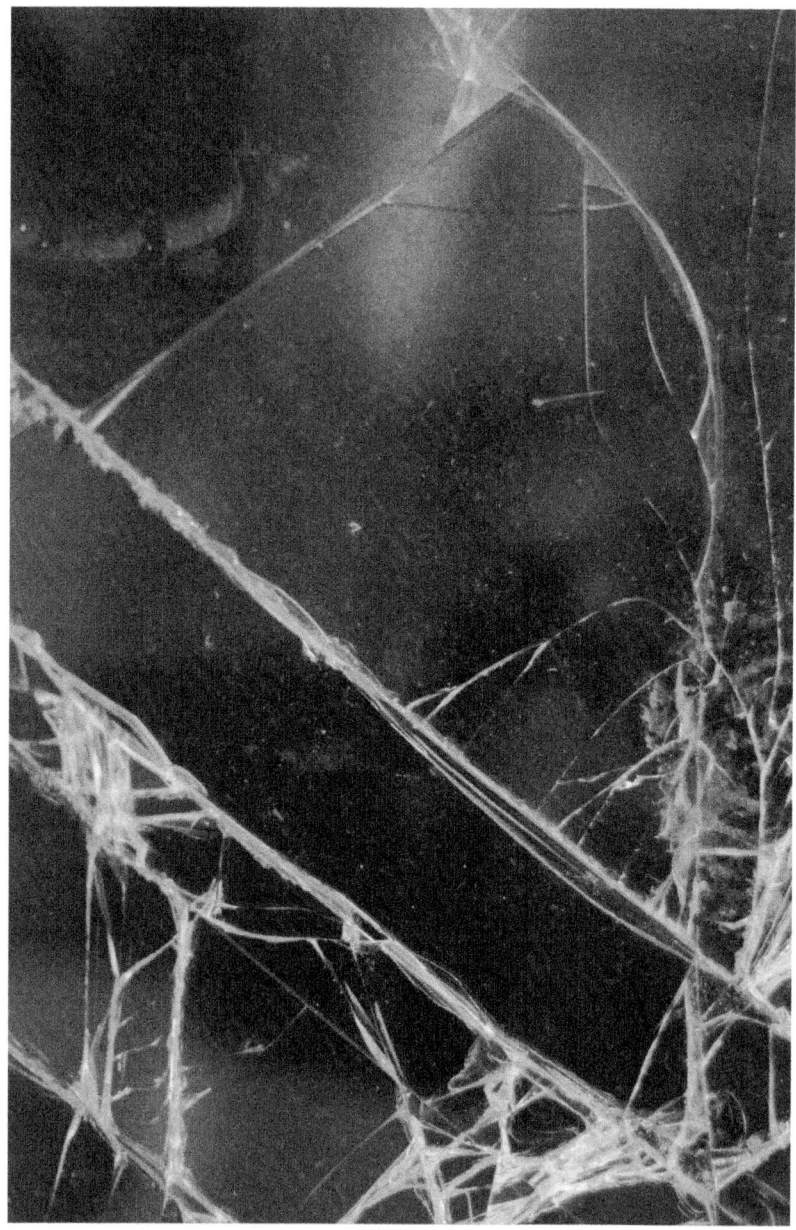

Fragment 33: An Extraordinary Coincidence

HALFWAY through the journey my heart feels as if it has stopped beating. I hang suspended above myself in the ether. I cannot believe what is happening, so precisely, as if it has been planned and timed with a stopwatch.

Carole, has dark, shoulder-length hair and is a couple of years older than me. She has only lived on Jersey for a short time. She tells me her brother used to be an actor. I latch on to something we have in common to make conversation. I tell her my brother is an actor too. Carole gives out a little more information. Her brother's girlfriend had been the trendy fashion designer Hilary Floyd.

At this point I consider leaping from the car and making a dash for safety. Carole's brother, I discover, is called John. I realise he is the same John who shared a flat in London with Tony and his ex-girlfriend Anne. The first time we met Tony talked in depth about John - how close they were, how they cut themselves, mixed their blood, and swore to be blood brothers. John had inherited a fortune at twenty-one and their friendship had ended.

We arrive at a small complex of apartments surrounded by fields. I am ushered into a comfortable living room, still full of misgivings. Staring out from a silver photograph frame on the mantelpiece is an extremely handsome young man.

"That's John, my brother," Carole says proudly.

Fragment 34: Pieces of the Jigsaw

I find myself enmeshed in the routine of looking after Carole's small daughters, aged two and three. The eldest is by a previous lover. She met Mike, her husband, at the Dorchester Hotel in London where he trained as a chef. She had been staying there with her mother and had fallen in love with him when he asked her to dance. She tells me he has stabilised her. She shows me the scars on her arm where she has slashed herself with a razor.

On my days off I write short stories and post them to Ken in the box at the carrefour. The rest of the time I deal with washing, ironing, feeding and amusing the little girls. I am happy being with them. They are uncomplicated.

When Mike is away on business I chat to Carole in the evenings. I discover that she was fostered out by her mother. She hadn't been brought into the family until she was in her late teens, when she also inherited money. She shows me the gold watch John bought her for her 21st birthday. It cost a staggering £1,000.

Her mother married an American who started with a stall and became a wealthy Manhattan jeweller. It is a complicated family history. When her mother finds out about my relationship with Tony she reveals that in his early teens he had stayed at her home in Maidenhead, at weekends and in the summer holidays. She fills in pieces of the jigsaw I had not been able to find.

She recalls how Tony had smashed a Regency mirror that stood in the hallway.

Fragment 35: Jimi Hendrix

I return home at Christmas with a large bottle of Christian Dior Eau de Toilette and tax-free gifts for my family. My dread of Tony has diminished. He has stopped phoning. I feel less intense. Something intangible between us has been severed.

I listen with George to the Bee Gees' single *New York Mining Disaster*, and on the flip side *I Can't See Nobody*. This new group is causing a sensation.

Clive has moved into a flat in King's Road. It is above a boutique. He has just finished filming an episode of *The Avengers*, in which he wrestles with Emma Peel on a diving board and is tossed into a swimming pool, after trying to shoot her.

He is wearing a white jumper and a perfect pair of jeans, and his dark, curly hair nearly reaches his shoulders. He is the epitome of cool and self-possession. He tells me how attractive actress Diane Rigg, who plays Emma Peel, is. She even says *fuck* with class.

A crowd of us go to see Jimi Hendrix perform at the Saville Theatre. He is stunning. He is like a Black Gypsy Dylan. He seems to float on to the stage. He reaches a climax with his first chord. The audience is full of trendy people. My mother comes too. She enjoys it but the powerful acoustics give her a migraine.

Weeks later, I catch Hendrix jamming at the UFO Club, off Tottenham Court Road. Members of London's underground movement meet here on Friday nights in a basement and stay until dawn. I also see Arthur Brown sing *Fire!* and set light to the top of his head.

In the advent of psychedelia Pink Floyd, the resident group, project slides. Colours burst into a frenzy of patterns. Evolving hippies in a euphoric love haze, stoned out of their minds.

Ken sends me to interview Jimi Hendrix for the first issue of a new magazine, *Go Girl - 'Everything on the bright side of the scene'*. I wake up with a terrible cold on the day of the assignment. London is chilly. It's raining. I meet Ken at the Marlborough Head and have several glasses of port and brandy, which he swears is the best remedy for a cold. By the time I reach my destination I am slightly tipsy.

I catch a cab with a photographer. We rendezvous at Jimi's manager's office and drive to a flat in a packed car. Jimi is staying in the Baker Street area, surrounded by henchmen who all seem highly amused.

Hendrix is shy, hides behind teasing me. He tells me one of his dislikes is girls wearing tights. I am wearing tights under my mini, like most of the female population who have abandoned stockings and suspenders. His henchmen snigger.

I pull out a tape recorder, something I have never used before and interview him in the question-and-answer style that later becomes a favourite with celebrity magazines. I kick off by asking his views on women.

"Women? Yeh, they're very nice." Jimi grins.

The fact that you've made it over here in England first?

"You know people say, 'they couldn't make it over in America so they had to come here,' but you know it wasn't exactly like this. Like when I was in the States most of the time I

was playing behind other groups. Like you don't really bring forward what you can do because it's somebody else's show first of all. This was except just before I came over here. I had this group see, just started to get on the scene together then. But it was only the Village scene, like a tight little circle."

Intend to stay based in England?

"Probably have to be based here right now but I don't really like to live anywhere for too long at a time to tell you the truth. I don't like to consider living here or living there or living anywhere. It's really more fun moving around, you know."

England and the English people?

"Oh it's great. The streets are like fairy tales. Some of them do you know. I don't like the mashed potatoes here. It's bad. Very bad food."

Time devoted to work?

"Almost all of it. Every single minute I'm thinking about music. Constantly. Sometimes you can't even sleep because you think about what you'd like to do tomorrow. It's the whole thing for me. I was about three of four years old when I first started thinking about music. I used to like violins and harps. I always liked music."

Music in the future?

"Right now we'd like to be known for our sound. That's one ambition. But there's so many other things. The goal that I might set for myself is completely unreachable, so you know, that's my life."

Dig anyone else on the pop scene?

"I know this probably sounds kinda weird you know but um the new scene that Eric Burdon has completely knocked me out. It's too much. I saw him at a club. Everything was happening and it didn't interfere, like when you have light shows for instance, well most of the time all you are is a voice for the lights, you're a slave to the lights. But he had the lights working with him. The scene he has now is really nice. I dig it. It's more original.

I quite naturally like a lot of the blues groups. You don't necessarily have to like a group for their ability to play, you might like them for their dynamics or the feeling they have regardless of how bad or good they sing. And so like I dig John Mayall. I dig watching him although I haven't particularly fallen in love with his records."

Temperament?

"It's very, very inconsistent. Like you go into different moods within a split second sometimes, which sometimes you can't help. You know a lot of times you say things, like if you say something bad to somebody like I was doing last night, the next thing you might say is nice. In other words you're very inconsistent. I'm very moody. I don't know exactly what's going to happen next."

Interests?

"I like science fiction. Yeh. Good science fiction. Then there are some things like I was getting together like outlines. Some rough ideas for things I'd like to do later if I was writing. I used to paint beforehand. But very seldom now. Art and music. It's about the same thing. Girls." He grins wickedly.

Astrology?

"I'm Sagittarius. It does interest me. We used to do that a long time ago. Now it's starting to catch on. Actually I might read things in the paper and get a few little books here and there but not necessarily live by it. I just want to see what it says about tomorrow and tomorrow I forget all about it. It's just interesting to read."

Clothes?

"I really dig 'em. That's what I spend most of my money on buying all these clothes and then they tear up and wind up missing and all that. The things I buy now you just can't wear them every day. I do but I might get hung up on a certain piece. I have all my clothes made because I'm a very deflected shape. You know very deformed. I mostly go to antique shops, find something a little kinda weird in an unorthodox place."

Difference in working in England and America?

"Well actually we've only worked over there once. Like, when we were there is about the same as over here. Like, as far as receptions, they really gave us a nice reception. Every place we played was a complete success. And there's really no difference at all except that they know more about us over here than they do over there. Now they've started to catch on to us over there. So, it's the time."

Is everything that is happening, happening in pop?

"Not necessarily no. Like spirituals are starting to come to the States. There are so many things happening too – Country and Western, Blues."

Musical influences?

"I listen to everything that's written. It keeps my interest. From rock to the Beatles to Muddy Waters to Elma James which is a blues guitar and singer. And I listen to Bob Dylan."

Bob Dylan?

"I was his manager with spots on the street you know. Like they're some people, like there's some songs that you do like if you're going to do somebody else's song most people do it and say, 'Well this is popular now. Well guess we'll do this,' but everybody knows that Like A Rolling Stone isn't popular now. It's a certain respect you might have. You know you don't do everybody's song and if you're going to do 'em well, like you don't necessarily have to copy it like. If you really dig the person and really really dig the song, well then you do it your own way. I like the way we do Rolling Stone myself."

Philosophy for life?

"Well like, let your mind and fancy roll on. You know."

Violent dislikes?

"You know I do have some but they'd have to happen before I could really recognise them. They don't bug me unless they really happen."

Communication musically?

"We try but sometimes there's so many things you might want to say in so little time you get almost like frustrated, like an old maid or something like that sometimes.

That's why you go into these different moods and are very temperamental. I can't help it because there are so many things I want to do. I don't ever think I'll get the chance to do all the things I really want to do so far as music wise."

Money?

"I'm so bad when it comes to money. I force myself to save it by not knowing it's around and not being able to get it any time I want. Because I store it away a lot of the time. Because I don't have too much value for money except for the things I want quite naturally."

Friends?

"Well I don't really know if I have friends or not. I mean the cats in the group and all this and Chas Chandler my manager and Jerry the road manager. Granny Goose, that's his nickname. Jerry Stickells – Granny Goose. Lot of people I talk to and all that. My eyes are very bad and sometimes you might go into a club and you might not see somebody and they might get all funny – 'Oh you're big time now, you won't talk to me.'

'I said hallo, I was thinking about something. I'm sorry.' Because you daydream a lot."

Fragment 36: A Degas Ballet Dancer

CLIVE'S pad attracts numerous visitors wanting to drop off for a smoke and listen to sounds. He is an extremist and begins to indulge in numerous joints, mostly of Lebanese hashish. He has huge chunks of it and the meticulous art of joint making becomes a serious business.

Dylan's *Blonde On Blonde* album travels out into the busy King's Road. I listen to *Sad Eyed Lady of the Lowlands* sharply aware of every nuance. Clive has stacks of records and books. He sits among these like a contemporary Jesus, surrounded by his disciples.

Clive and friends experiment with slides and one night project their own light show out of the window on the buildings at the back of the flat. One weekend a group of us pile into a van and drive up the motorways to Wales on a spontaneous pilgrimage to the grave of Dylan Thomas at Laugharne, where Dylan found inspiration for *Under Milk Wood*.

We bow before the simple wooden cross which marks the spot where he is buried and run across the deserted beach beneath screeching gulls. We drink pints of draft Guinness.

On the return journey one of Clive's friends, a young photographer, asks me out. David Scott has high cheekbones, a full mouth, and blue almond eyes. He has dark hair with a long fringe. He is sensitive and refined.

Ken knows immediately he is introduced to David that he has been to a public school. Although he can't hear him speak, he can tell from his body language.

David's mother, Ruth, lives in a mews off King's Road and makes props for theatres. She has an original Degas bronze of a ballet dance on her coffee table. His grandmother's house is in a prestigious square behind Oxford Street and has an elevator. I spot an original

Lowry on the wall. David's grandmother rings a bell for her maid to bring us tea.

Fragment 37: Waterloo Sunset

DAVID'S more humble abode is a flat near Barons Court Station.

He is an aspiring photographer and has a darkroom with all sorts of equipment. In the evenings he works for a minicab company taking calls, to top up his allowance from his father, Richard Scott who is Washington Correspondent for the Guardian. He has divorced Ruth and remarried. David's great grandfather was CP Scott, legendary editor of the Manchester Guardian and his godfather is the famous cartoonist Osbert Lancaster. He has one of his original cartoons on the wall. David is most unassuming and never brags about his prestigious background.

He has one black suit, one pair of brown Hush Puppies, and a purple shirt which he wears with a boldly patterned tie. He has not been at all spoilt, despite his Gordonstoun education. He is attractive but not in the least conceited. He is soft, gentle, and sensual.

My parents are delighted I am seeing David who has beautiful manners. If he brings me flowers, he also brings a bunch for my mother.

He takes some shots of me posed by an old-fashioned post-box in Cheyne Walk. He makes them grainy. I no longer look sad. My features are harder.

We listen, over and over, to the Kinks' *Waterloo Sunset*.

I don't know what I want, or what is good for me.

Fragment 38: Blood Brothers

CAROLE writes to me from Jersey. They have bought a small hotel in St Helier. She invites me to go for a week at Easter.

David takes me to Gatwick in one of the minicabs. I wear purple tights and silver shoes, a black velvet jacket over a deep pink shirt and a hipster skirt. My purple boater won't stay on because of the wind.

When I arrive Carole warns me John is staying.

"Don't mention Tony. He doesn't want to talk about him. It's part of his life that he wants to forget," she warns.

I don't intend to make John feel uncomfortable. I'm not even sure I want to meet him. I haven't seen Tony for six months. I am getting on with my life.

John is acting the part of a barman. He is wearing an exquisitely tailored, dark blue suit and a bow tie. He looks as if he is in an advertisement in *Vogue*. He is tall and has great presence.

I smile, sit on a bar stall. He conjures up an exotic cocktail and pushes it across to me. Then he slips me a piece of paper with writing on it. *DOES HE STILL WRITE LIKE THIS?*

I stare down at handwriting that is identical to Tony's Gothic script.

A long, intense conversation follows. I discover John loves him as much as I do, understands him, sees him in exactly the same way. *I share my craziness with Tony's blood brother.*

John's second wife is a beautiful blonde Australian. They have a tiny blonde daughter. I am surprised when John invites me, a few days later, to be their nanny. I tell him firmly that I have commitments in London.

I fly away from the island, and never hear from any of them again.

Fragment 39: Something Invisible

TONY was so full of life in the morning, whistling and pulling on his donkey jacket and thick woollen socks, making toast and uncapping pints of milk.

One of my friends reads in a newspaper that he dragged a motorist out of a car, tore his sweater, smashed his glasses. He wrestled with two policemen.

I dream of him. I am frightened, trying to escape. I dream of him. We make love. I see him in a dream but he does not see me. I see him again and he speaks to me. I tell him how much I still care.

I dream I go to an old house and Tony is sitting in a leather chair. I approach him but he does not recognise me. He comes through mists still unable to identify me. He turns into a Black woman with an American accent. She is working for Oxfam and writes me a cheque.

Someone spots him wearing a gigantic sandwich board advertising furniture.

I see Tony from a high window on a foggy day. He is walking slowly, holding a carrier bag. His eyes and ears are fixed to, tuned to, something invisible. I watch him, until he disappears...

YOU WRITE ME A LETTER FROM KUWAIT.

YOU HAVE BECOME A CHARACTER IN A BOOK TO ME; A KEROUAC; A MAILER; A YOUNGER HENRY MILLER. WE HAVE WRITTEN YOU INTO A BOOK BETWEEN US; AN EVER-LIVING BOOK WHICH ENDS AS SOON AS I CHOOSE TO CLOSE THE MEMORIES THAT BIND IT, AND IT BEGINS AGAIN IN BEAUTIFUL SPIRITUAL PARAGRAPHS THAT I CONTINUE TO FEED UPON.

YOU SAY YOU ARE NOT COMING BACK FOR A LONG TIME. YOU ARE GOING INTO EGYPT, DOWN INTO SWEDEN. YOU SAY YOU ARE LOCKED UP AGAIN, BUT NOT FOR LONG. YOU ARE MORE OPTIMISTIC THAN BEFORE. YOU STOLE SOME CANVAS TO MAKE A TENT. WHY NOT?

YOU SAY, WHEN YOU REALISE THAT YOU COULD HAVE DONE ALL THIS BEFORE, THIS TRAVELLING, YOU COULD KILL YOURSELF. YOU SUGGEST THAT MAYBE I'LL JOIN YOU IN PARIS OR BRUSSELS WHEN IT'S WARMER. BUT I WILL NEVER COME, ALTHOUGH I AM WITH YOU, HIKING THROUGH HOT AND COLD, FLOATING SHADOW-CONTINENTS, TOWARDS INFINITY, AMONG A MILLION SUNS.

YES, YOU HAVE KILLED *US* AND I HAVE KILLED *YOU*. WE ARE ALIVE, ETERNALLY IN EACH OTHER'S ARMS, THOUGH NEVER TOUCHING OR SEEING, FOR NOTHING THAT REALLY *IS* IS EVER *WAS*.

BETWEEN THE BROKEN GLASS OF US, OF EVERYTHING, THE PEOPLE PLAY. AND I PLAY WITH THEM, FOR BROKEN GLASS STILL SHINES.

Actor Dominic Herman-Day trained at the Sylvia Young Theatre School and in his early teens became a pioneer YouTuber with thousands of followers. He works in films and television, and is a Street Photographer.

ACKNOWLEDGEMENTS

Many thanks to mega Aquarian **Dominic Herman-Day** *for capturing the stunning, cutting-edge broken glass images which he found on the streets of London. Also thank you to my dear mother* **Irene -** *a true Aquarian and years ahead of her time - for her sense of humour, for encouraging me, and for tolerating us! And a tribute to another amazing Aquarian,* **Geoff Beale,** *whose support and generosity of spirit knows no bounds.*

Extracts: *Nerves And Their Cure and Psychology's Impact On The Christian Faith by C Edward Barker, George Allen & Unwin, 1960, 1964 -- my interviews Sixties magazines Big Beat, Boyfriend, Fabulous, Trend and Go Girl -- the original Between The Broken Glass The People Play, published in New Writers 8, Calder & Boyars 1968 and in Red Dust One, Red Dust Inc, New York 1970, which gave me a framework for this longer novella.*

Photo Page 57   Clive by Sixties, era-defining photographer Lewis Morley

Cover Photo   Christine by Feri Lucas

OTHER BOOKS by CHRISTINE DAY

A Unicorn Danced In The Woods, The Name On The Mirror,

A Retro Collection of 70's/80's Short Stories, Jappy A Spiritual Cat

www.christineday.co.uk   www.christinedaywriter.weebly.com

Printed in Great Britain
by Amazon

44926913R00098